Debating the Industrial Revolution

DEBATES IN WORLD HISTORY

Series Editor: Peter N. Stearns, George Mason University, USA

Bloomsbury's *Debates in World History* series presents students with accessible primers to the key debates in the field of world history, from classic debates, such as the great divergence, through to cutting-edge current developments. These are short, argumentative texts that will encourage undergraduate level history students to engage in the practice of doing history.

Published:
Debating the Industrial Revolution, Peter N. Stearns

Forthcoming:
Debating Revolutions in World History, Jack R. Censer

Debating the Industrial Revolution

PETER N. STEARNS

Bloomsbury Academic
An imprint of Bloomsbury Publishing Plc

B L O O M S B U R Y
LONDON · NEW DELHI · NEW YORK · SYDNEY

Bloomsbury Academic

An imprint of Bloomsbury Publishing Plc

50 Bedford Square	1385 Broadway
London	New York
WC1B 3DP	NY 10018
UK	USA

www.bloomsbury.com

BLOOMSBURY and the Diana logo are trademarks of Bloomsbury Publishing Plc

First published 2015

© Peter N. Stearns, 2015

British Library Cataloguing-in-Publication Data

A catalogue record for this book is available from the British Library.

ISBN:	HB:	978-1-4725-8936-1
	PB:	978-1-4725-8935-4
	ePDF:	978-1-4725-8937-8
	ePub:	978-1-4725-8938-5

Library of Congress Cataloging-in-Publication Data

A catalog record for this book is available from the Library of Congress.

Series: Debates in World History

Typeset by RefineCatch Limited, Bungay, Suffolk
Printed and bound in India

Contents

1

Why debate the Industrial Revolution?

The Industrial Revolution was one of the truly big changes in modern world history—arguably, the greatest single transformation in the human experience over the past 250 years. The revolution's core centered on the development of new technologies, plus a new, more disciplined organization of labor, both based on the application of new energy sources to manufacturing and transportation. The creation of the factory system had sweeping impacts ranging from living standards, to the nature of war, to family structure and purpose, and even to artistic expression. With industrialization societies became more urban, considerably wealthier (at least overall), with a dramatic new demographic structure based on low birth rates and higher life expectancy. Industrial change affected virtually every aspect of human and social life.

Agricultural economies had lasted, in most parts of the world, for several thousand years, and in a few cases longer. But almost in the blink of an eye, in just two or three generations, they began to be overturned. With this, the average person became not a farmer, but a city dweller. Factories, not households, produced the greatest number of goods. Because of their new importance, machines began to receive more attention than human workers did. Why did such huge changes occur? What would motivate people to accept, much less to introduce, so many innovations? What, in sum, were the key causes of developments that began to shape the modern world?

The contrasts between industrialized societies and their earlier agricultural counterparts are massive. Only the much earlier transition from hunting and gathering to agriculture offers remotely comparable scope, in the human experience. While not everything altered—for example, in the persistence of major religions—even older elements operated within a substantially novel, and challenging, industrial framework.

As a phenomenon, the Industrial Revolution was global from the outset, though its geography was complex. Early industrialization occurred in only a few places, which in itself had radical impact on the balance of power around the world. But even from this limited base industrialization transformed the world economy, with new demands for resources and markets literally throughout the globe. It quickly affected the environment, not only in the smoky centers of factory industry but also in places like Brazil or Africa where new needs for products like rubber or cotton led to damaging patterns of land use. Above all, industrialization in one place, because of its implications for military and economic power, quickly spurred attention in other places, with efforts to replicate the process shaping modern history of countries as diverse as Egypt and Japan during the nineteenth century, and then becoming part of world history more generally in the century that followed.

The process of industrialization was not fully or formally identified until the later nineteenth century. Before then, many workers certainly knew that their lives were changing—and often deteriorating—and many businessmen began praising aspects of the new order. But scholarly attention to industrialization took a while to develop, partly because relevant observers were more accustomed to examining political or diplomatic patterns rather than changes rooted in new economic forms and new technologies. Even today, many history surveys remain more comfortable with wars or political revolutions than with sweeping changes like industrialization. In fairness, industrialization does present at least one challenge: while the process is substantial and comprehensive, it takes several decades before it is in any sense complete. This makes it difficult to fit industrialization neatly into the kind of chronology many history books favor, with decade-by-decade accounts of major events and personalities.

By now, of course, despite the special features involved, the Industrial Revolution has generated a large scholarly literature. Economic historians deal with changes in production levels and trade patterns. A substantial part of the field of the history of technology has revolved around the emergence and steady evolution of new machines. Social historians, though a slightly more recent chorus, seek to investigate the impacts of industrialization of various aspects of human life, from living standards to work experiences to an impressive alteration of leisure habits, with due attention to differences in social class and gender.

The combination of major significance and substantial and varied scholarship means, predictably, that the Industrial Revolution is also a field for pressing historical debate. There is some discussion, first, about what the Industrial Revolution was and whether the term "revolution" is really appropriate; we will cover this angle in the next chapter, because it contributes to a sense of what the whole process was about. On the whole, however, this is not a particularly revealing or urgent discussion, because in fact wide agreement exists both on the revolutionary nature of the change, and on what its basic components were, starting with the core technologies.

At the other extreme there has always been vivid argument about industrialization's effects, and whether industrial societies and economies are better or worse than their agricultural predecessors in terms of human impact. This kind of evaluation is absolutely essential as part of our whole sense of the nature of modern experience, and we will refer to it again in the final chapter. The debate here has a few quite specific foci—like a bitter, though now dated, argument about changes in living standards during British industrialization—but it ranges far more broadly into assessments of growing materialism, environmental quality, the changes in family life and so on. Even mental illness factors in: do industrial conditions promote more mental illness and/or make mental illness more problematic? (The answers are probably yes and yes.) But while these discussions deserve serious attention, they are also inherently diffuse, involving many value judgments as well as more standard historical data and considerations. They do not organize the most focused historical inquiry.

This means that, finally, it is a third target for debate that warrants particular attention, and serves as the subject of most of the chapters in this book. The spotlight here is on *causation*: what set of factors can possibly explain why industrialization took shape, why people embraced, or had to embrace, such radically new ways of doing things.

In the case of the previous great change in the human framework—the replacement of hunting and gathering by agriculture—we can only guess at the factors that impelled people to transform their lives, for the records are too scarce, particularly the kinds of records that allow some assessment of motivations. With industrialization, however, records abound, including memoirs, government reports, business archives, material artifacts including the machines themselves, and much more. Abundance does not settle debate, and indeed may encourage it, because there are inevitably different ways of evaluating the same materials or varied choices of some materials over others. We will see, for example, how early assessments of causation have been reshaped simply by more focused research. But at least there is a considerable empirical platform.

Causation is virtually impossible to ignore in human history; we always want to know what prompted the big changes of the past, whether the issue is a great war, a revolution, a novel religion, or a dramatic shift in economic systems. Probing causes helps us better understand the phenomenon itself. Rather than simply describing the Industrial Revolution—listing the new inventions or the rise of manufactured products—if we can figure out *why* the new factories and machines came into being we will be much closer to understanding their meaning and the purposes they were meant to serve. Debates over the causes of the Industrial Revolution, as we will see, force some decisions about types of factors that are most likely to induce fundamental human changes. Can rather narrow factors—for example, a decline in available wood for fuel in Great Britain—cause great transformations, or must we look for a far wider set of impulses? Or another option: what is the role of government? We will see that some historians choose to ignore government altogether, in explaining the Industrial Revolution, while others see it as fundamental. Why do such differences in explanation persist?

For while historical causation adds meaning, it also poses a challenging analytical assignment. This is true with virtually any causation discussion, and certainly with one attached to such a major transformation as industrialization. The fact is that though historians normally delight in exploring causation, they can never prove their findings definitively. That's why causes, though intriguing, so often provoke debate, whether it's a specific question, like "What caused the First World War?" or a more diffuse problem like the factors prompting industrialization. This is why—to be candid—when you're done with this book you should still have some questions. You will have a much better sense of what industrialization was and is all about; but you will still find room for debate.

And feel free to explore one other basic question at the end: have historians improved our understanding of why industrial revolutions happen, even as they continue to argue? I think the answer is yes, but you may decide otherwise.

While exploring the causes of the Industrial Revolution links to other efforts to explain historical change, it embraces one other element that adds further spice: this is a debate with practical policy implications, in addition to its scholarly significance. In this sense, this book offers a double payoff: it presents a really important set of historical explanations around a moving force in the modern experience, and it explores guidelines for contemporary economic development policy.

The implications for policy became clear early on. For once Britain began to industrialize (in the late eighteenth century) and even more, when it began to be obvious (by the early nineteenth century) that its power and prosperity were expanding as a result, other business and political leaders began to wonder what they had to do to get into the game. Clearly, they needed to get their hands on some of the new technology, but might more be involved? The answer to this very practical question really required at least an implicit effort to figure out what causes were in play: what qualities did Britain have that other countries should generate, in order to have a similar industrial outcome?

The challenge might not be directly stated as a causation issue, but that is what it was. To take an early example: a new leader in Egypt, Muhammad Ali, clearly realized that his country was falling behind Western economic levels in the early nineteenth century, and he wanted to remedy the situation. And he knew that, in the Egyptian case, it was not enough to bring in some new machines. At least four other components were essential: a supply of factory labor; funds to pay for initial industrial ventures; major improvements in technical education for a new elite; and, though this final component was related, new types of bureaucrats, different from the traditional leadership groups, interested in industrial expansion. Muhammad Ali used his own methods to meet the first two needs, forcing workers into factories and raising taxes and the government's role in trade to generate capital. But he also sent many Egyptians to gain technical expertise in West European schools and deliberately displaced the traditional elite, in order to meet the requirements in expertise and leadership. Muhammad Ali had not studied the still-new Industrial Revolution in any formal sense, and his industrialization effort ultimately failed in part because he complicated it with military ambitions; but his diagnosis remains interesting as an early example of the practical need to come to terms with causation.

The story would be multiplied later on, as the drawbacks of falling behind in industrialization became ever-clearer. By the 1860s Japan was sending observers to industrial countries, to try to ascertain what made them tick; and the results helped organize a host of reforms that would indeed begin to bring Japan into the ranks of industrial economies. It was vital to know what had to be changed in Japanese institutions and culture in order to begin to catch up with industrial leaders; national independence itself might be at stake, in this age of Western imperialism. Figuring out causation was far more than an academic exercise.

Fast forward to the twentieth century, particularly after the Second World War. By this point not only national leaders but also policy scholars became deeply interested in further diagnosing the causes of industrialization, but also the causes of lagging responses to industrialization, as part of addressing pressing problems in regional economic development. Why were some nations, eager in principle to industrialize, actually having difficulties? What factors were particularly difficult to replicate in promoting industrial revolutions? A whole field of development economics explored questions of this sort, using historical analysis but contributing to it at the same time.

By now, early in the twenty-first century, with the majority of world regions developing successful industrial economies, the policy aspects of industrial causation may have become somewhat less pressing. Most societies have now at least initiated this massive process of change, which means that they have figured out a causation formula that works for them. But there are still regions left out, and the recency of industrialization means that even success stories like China or Brazil are still reasonably fresh in memory, with some concerns about the possibility of slipping back from current levels of economic achievement. Causation is still a contemporary issue, as well as a challenging historical puzzle.

The next chapter will discuss what the Industrial Revolution was about. As already indicated, there's some debate here, particularly around the quantitative measures that demonstrate the pace and range of development that make a "real" industrial revolution as opposed to more modest kinds of change. The chapter also must pick up another characteristic issue in dealing with industrialization, in conveying some of the human aspect of the change, the real people involved and (briefly) some of what they experienced.

Some of the early explanations of the Industrial Revolution are reviewed in Chapter 3, beginning with the British historian who first used the term. Briefly reviewing some of the history accomplishes two goals. First, obviously, it introduces some of the components that any causation debate has to consider: these include government role and policy, labor supply and training, and the role of invention. Second, this provides a baseline for the more recent debates over causation, suggesting what elements survive or recur in analysis but also where newer discoveries or emphases have really altered the picture. We will see for example that the role of consumer demand, now an important component in some explanations, was simply ignored in the earlier formulations, while the place of culture, while not formally identified as has become common more recently, did gain some attention.

Chapter 4 centers on the target of any significant historical inquiry into the Industrial Revolution, the case of Britain as the world's first industrializer. Some historical explanations begin and end with Britain, as if later developments elsewhere offer no analytical challenge; this is not the approach we will take. But because Britain was first it logically involves some special ingredients, and historians continue to debate what these were.

The next two chapters continue to deal with Britain, but also other cases of fairly early industrialization that followed the British example, in Western Europe and the United States. This wider geographical framework raises some comparative issues beyond the examination of Britain alone. It also allows historians to explore human factors that early industrializers may have shared that were not for the most part captured in some of the original explanations of the Industrial Revolution. While no single person ever caused industrialization, even in a single place, people did play a role, as industrializers, workers, policymakers, and these are factors that need to be worked into the causation debates.

Branching off from this, in Chapter 6, are special topics around the role of education and the emergence of new kinds of consumerism, both of which now contribute to the exploration of industrial origins.

The geographical framework is broadened more fully in Chapters 7 and 8. The Industrial Revolution ultimately was not just a British or even a Western development. Looking at cases outside the direct Western orbit forces another set of comparative issues: to what extent were later industrializations different from the initial versions, to what extent do some of the same features apply? The same expansion allows some causation tests: do these additional cases on the whole highlight a separate set of factors, compared to British and Western precedents, or do they actually help confirm some of the priorities already identified?

Chapter 9 further extends the geographical and chronological framework. Industrial revolutions continue to occur, and while their greater frequency suggests that the process has become easier, it remains true that some regions move faster than others and so some distinctive causes are still involved. One of the key reasons to deal with causation debates involves the extent to which, ultimately, they address a global process, not just a British or Western change. This expansion complicates the causation analysis to some extent, but it links it to some of the more important developments in the world today.

The final chapter recaps some of the key issues in the assessment of causation, and raises some final questions for consideration.

The effort to figure out what causes an industrial revolution has real significance. It invites us to explain one of the great transformations of our time. It forces us to think about what kinds of factors motivate or compel people to engage in sometimes exciting—but often very intimidating innovations—a classic opportunity to figure out what makes human beings tick in shifting environments. And of course this kind of historical analysis may help us understand what still should be done to create conditions for some of the remaining less-industrial societies to make a fuller transformation.

And—for sheer mental stimulation—there is no question that the debates over industrial causation are challenging. A host of combinations are worth considering, amid an impressive range of possibilities. Discussion opportunities abound, and each of the following chapters highlights one or more leading targets. The main point centers on figuring out how to sort the various explanations, how to separate the more plausible from the less plausible options, or how to combine data with logical analysis. In the process many readers will gain some additional information about the Industrial Revolution in a global framework. But always, critical analysis, not disruptive detail, is the crucial target.

For further discussion

Here are some initial issues to keep an eye on in considering debates over the Industrial Revolution.

(1) Most discussions of the causes of industrialization do not place a great deal of emphasis on the special role of individual people, what historians often call the "great man" approach. All sorts of individuals played a leading role in industrial revolutions. A few pioneering business entrepreneurs and inventors probably top the list, but there are political leaders and social reformers as well, and even some exemplary workers. But most explanations of industrialization assume that if these particular individuals had not been around, someone else would have performed the same creative functions; there was no special genius involved, just individuals responding to broader factors. This applies even to some of the key inventors—like James Watt—who perfected the first steam engine for manufacturing. No individual ever fully planned an industrial revolution; the phenomenon was too vast to be attributed even to a creative genius. Biographies, as a result, do not figure prominently in analyzing causes. (Collective biographies, however, that group types of contributors, are another matter; we will see that a number of approaches work hard to capture a human element.) Individual stories illustrate factors and motivations, but not how the process was generated. But does this make the Industrial Revolution too anonymous? Should a greater part of the debate over industrial causation give credit to exceptional individuals? These are issues to test in assessing the explanations that have developed, and that we will be exploring in the following chapters. What challenges are involved in assuming that large, perhaps impersonal forces are responsible for major changes like industrialization? How, if at all, do we account for human agency?

(2) What are some of the key issues to consider in tackling a big problem in historical causation? There are several components here that are worth thinking about in advance.

   (a) For example: what's the difference between a correlation and a cause? It has recently been pointed out that divorce rates have been going down in the United States in recent decades while margarine consumption has been rising. Here's an easy case in which correlation almost certainly does not help an explanation. Can you think of other historical cases where correlations pose a problem, where relationships are more plausible than with margarine and divorce. And can you anticipate any correlation issues in trying to explain the Industrial Revolution?

   (b) Another example: what's the difference between a precondition and a cause? Britain's abundant rivers undoubtedly facilitated industrialization, but did they cause it? What are the issues in this case? And again, can you think of other precondition-active cause dilemmas?

   (c) And finally: what is the role of cultural or political bias in shaping historical explanations? We will see that, for the Industrial Revolution, current beliefs about economic policy undoubtedly affect the selection of historical causes. Cultural bias may enter in as well, particularly when Western historians examine factors involved in explaining industrialization or its absence in regions outside the West. Can we control for this factor, or is it a valid part of the analytical process? Does our understanding of the role of the State in prompting industrial revolutions contribute to our evaluation of government policy today? Are we still tempted to give too much credit to "Western values" in explaining industrial success?

Discussing some of the analytical components in historical causation—correlation; precondition; the roles of individuals and larger forces; the relationship to contemporary policy issues—is worthwhile in advance. The issues will carry directly into the following chapters.

2

Pinpointing the Industrial Revolution:

Features, times, and places

The Industrial Revolution is a definable process, but there is no question that it is less clear cut than some of the more familiar developments in history like wars or regime change. Debates over the causes of the First World War, for example, do not need to linger over the question of what the war was. But industrialization, though arguably far more important, lacks this kind of precision: it did not organize around a single set of events. As a result, causation debates require some preliminary characterizations. It is impossible reasonably to probe what caused a phenomenon, without an initial definition of what the phenomenon was. After this, the debates over causes and their variety will add further to the understanding of what the Industrial Revolution was all about—again—this kind of analysis always enhances historical description; but we need a clear sketch prior to addressing the challenge of explanation. The same sketch will suggest some important complexities, and indeed a recurrent debate over definitions and criteria.

This chapter, briefly outlining the main features of what the Industrial Revolution was all about, also highlights three sets of issues that inevitably spill over into the causation debates. First: are there ways precisely to measure industrial revolutions, to distinguish them for example from lesser kinds of change or mere pilot projects that set up a new factory or two but left most of the economy untouched?

Second: what was the human side of industrialization? How did this process involve, excite or offend businessmen, workers, consumers, or simple observers?

And third: why is geography such a challenge? When we talk about industrial revolutions, why must we linger on Britain but why, also, must we clearly go beyond the British case?

We'll start with a basic definition, but turn quickly to the questions of measuring the process; seeing the process as an intensely, often unpleasantly, human experience; and dealing with the knotty problem of geography.

The central features

The Industrial Revolution hinged on the application of new sources of power—primarily, fossil fuel power, though new uses of water power could also contribute—to manufacturing and transportation. For over a century, industrialization depended primarily on the power of the steam engine, to drive manufacturing machinery but also new forms of shipping and the railway. With new sources of power, increasingly replacing the muscles of humans and animals, key activities could be massively accelerated, volume greatly expanded. Far more goods could be produced, and more materials and output hauled to and from production sites.

Several other changes closely attached to the basic shift in power source. Manufacturing equipment had to be transformed, to allow more processes to be handled automatically, thus allowing transmission from the steam engines. In initial industrialization, some of these technological changes actually began to be devised and introduced before the connection to steam power. Cloth weaving offers a clear example. Traditionally, hand workers had to manipulate thread in two directions, up and down and across, in order to make cloth. But toward the middle of the eighteenth century a new device, the flying shuttle, literally revolutionized the weaving looms. Now, thread could be moved crosswise automatically, with the weaver simply pumping a foot pedal to activate the shuttle. This meant, even without the application of a new power source, a given manual weaver could increase output by about 50 percent. Similar gains were devised in other areas, such as spinning. Other early inventions, not directly attached to the steam engine, included using coal and coke, rather than charcoal, in smelting iron; again, there were independent opportunities here for expanded output, for with coke furnaces could be enlarged.

A second feature of industrialization, then, centered on a wider set of technological innovations, particularly in manufacturing, that challenged traditional methods and heightened production. When these were combined with the steam engine, the results, obviously, would be further magnified. Recurrent technological change became part of the industrialization process.

Technology linked to a third basic feature: the expansion of the factory system. Factories—the accumulation of many workers under one roof, with a more formal organization of labor and supervision included—were not brand new. But they had not been typical in manufacturing, which centered rather on small craft shops or home production. With new equipment, and particularly with steam engines, factories became more essential, because workers had to be clustered around the power source: steam power could not be transmitted very far. It turned out, however, that factories had their own contributions to make to increasing manufacturing output. With factories, labor could become more specialized—semi-skilled, not highly skilled workers were characteristic, and they were cheaper on average—and supervision could become more intense. Even without steam engines, the results of these organizational changes, though often unpleasant for many workers, benefitted production.

New power sources (for transportation as well as manufacturing), a wider array of new technologies for production, and new forms of work organization were core features of the Industrial Revolution. They generated a fourth definable feature: a rapid expansion of output in industrialized sectors, and a steady advance in the importance of manufacturing and related services over agriculture in the economy as a whole. These four criteria, closely interrelated, capture the essence of what the Industrial Revolution was all about, creating the foundation for the wider transformations industrialization would generate, for example in rapid rates of urbanization and related alterations of class structure.

Initial complexities

Without undoing the basic definition, it is important to indicate some problems attached. The criteria are sound, but their emergence involves some challenges in historical analysis.

The challenge of timing

Most obviously, the Industrial Revolution takes some time to develop—typically several decades—from clear beginnings to a substantial reworking of the economy. At any given point in this process, but particularly in the early phases, it is not always easy to be sure that systematic industrialization is occurring. Large, essentially traditional sectors in the economy, not only in agriculture but also in craft production, will continue to operate; indeed, sometimes they even expand at first, because of new opportunities created by industrialization. Building construction, for example, was not greatly transformed by early industrialization in places like Britain; technologies did not change much in this sector until later. But new buildings were vital in the growth of factories and industrial cities, which meant that craft work would actually grow for a time, though not at as rapid a rate as the factory labor force. Similarly, many people remained in agriculture, and while production changes might occur here they would be far less sweeping than in the factory sectors.

The gradual, prolonged unfolding of industrialization, and the continued presence of older economic forms, in turn can complicate the identification of the causes of change. Since the buildup of new technologies and organizations is drawn out, at what point do decisive new factors enter in? Is it really a revolution when many people, on the farms or in craft sites, maintain lives not much changed from those of their grandparents?

Identifying an industrial revolution depends on steady expansion and impact of initially small sectors. By the end of the "revolutionary" process—as many as 60–80 years after clear beginnings of technological change and the rise of factories—a substantial sector of the manufacturing economy will be operating on the largely new bases. Persistent, cumulative impact is the name of the game. And by the later stages of the transformation, even more traditional sectors will begin to reflect the results. Agriculture must change enough to generate more food for factory cities; craft work, while it may persist, has to take on new qualities in order to remain competitive. The result is a real technological and organizational revolution, even if it takes two or three generations to complete.

By the same token—and this is crucial to causation discussions as well—it must be possible to distinguish between the introduction of a handful of factories with steam engines, and a real industrial transformation. From the middle of the nineteenth century onward—and even a bit earlier in the case of Muhammad Ali's Egypt—a number of governments or businessmen were capable of copying Britain or other Western countries in setting up a few factories and laying out a few railway lines. By 1850 pilot projects of this sort—including short rail lines—could be found in Russia and several Latin American countries, as well as Egypt. These might be important changes, and they certainly reflected the global reach of early industrialization, but they did not usually signal a real industrial revolution. Only if initial pilot efforts introduced steady and systematic change, in technology and organization and in the rate and level of manufacturing, was a full industrialization process underway. For all the complexities in defining an industrial revolution given the long timeframe involved, it is possible to separate the whole process from other interesting but less transformational developments.

One other aspect of the gradual quality of the Industrial Revolution attaches directly to causation discussions: early industrialization involved radical change, but not always quite as extensive as we might imagine based on contemporary patterns. Steam engines were really new—there is no backing away from the revolutionary claim—but early machines were relatively small, which might limit the adjustments needed at least to some extent. They did not even eliminate the need for considerable physical strength in some factory jobs, for it took time for all processes to be automated. Even more important, most early factories and machine shops themselves were modest by contemporary standards. They were bigger than traditional craft shops and family production units—again there was serious change involved—but they often involved 20–30 workers, not the thousands that would be attached to factories later in the industrial process. Here too, adjustments were real; and there were some larger units even then. But for many workers and employers the innovation challenge was slightly less great than might be assumed, and therefore the causes of change might be slightly less sweeping than might otherwise be indicated. The complexity of machines and organizations would grow steadily as the Industrial Revolution proceeded—another inherent aspect of the process historically—but there was some time to adjust to the changes in scale. Again, gradualness does not detract from ultimately revolutionary qualities and consequences, but it can and should affect the assessment of initial causation. We still need some "big" causes, but how big?

The timing of industrial revolutions thus involves several challenges. It is vital to be able to identify when a definable industrialization process begins; causes cannot be discussed without agreeing on chronology. Yet the process will extend over several decades, which means that revolutionary aspects may not be visible too quickly. Nevertheless, a real industrial revolution can and must be distinguished from less decisive developments, like an early factory or two, which do not turn out to generate steady change.

Finally, regarding timing: the case of British industrialization, clearly the first to occur, may well involve a particularly long incubation period. Most historians argue that a British industrial revolution was certainly underway by the 1770s or 1780s, when the steam engine was introduced to manufacturing, though we will encounter one argument that has the inception later. By 1850, even though sectors of the economy lagged, a basic transformation had occurred, signaled among other things by the fact that Britain by this point had become half urban, the first such marker in human history. But key elements of change in technology and labor organization actually began earlier, as in the invention of the flying shuttle in the 1730s. At what point then, should we say that an irreversible change was beginning to occur? At what point do causes need to be identified? We will see that debates over causation, particularly for Britain, inevitably embrace this discussion of inception.

The challenge of measurement: debating the data

Characterizing the Industrial Revolution, and dealing with the crucial issues of timing and location, inevitably generated a number of discussions among historians. A key argument featured an attempt to challenge the very idea of industrial revolution, based on the inherent gradualness of the process of change. Growing interest in quantitative data added fuel to the fire, for some of the measurements seemed surprisingly modest.

The classic idea of the Industrial Revolution, as we have seen, featured fairly sweeping changes, with new technologies being applied in a number of sectors, and with dramatic results including the rapid urbanization of growing sectors of the population and rising overall production levels. This approach obviously encouraged causation analysis: what combination of factors could possibly explain such massive change? But what if the change turned out to be less massive?

For by the 1970s a variety of economic historians began to cut through the generalizations and challenge the approach. They argued that a closer look at British data suggested a far less dynamic picture. Specifically, they sought to prove that only a few industries were in any sense rapidly or substantially transformed, and that most of the British economy grew at most gradually, while retaining essentially traditional technologies and organizational forms. They also pointed out that even when growth occurred it was inconsistent and frequently interrupted; there was no steady march of progress. A few went so far as to question whether the term industrial revolution made any sense at all.

This new school also disputed the idea that the Industrial Revolution "took off" from some purely traditional past. An American scholar, W.W. Rostow, had emphasized the sharp contrasts between Britain's earlier economy and its new industrial advances, as he ventured a model of key stages of revolutionary development leading to a point at which automatic further progress was assured. Rostow was separately criticized for oversimplifying industrial patterns and overemphasizing the extent to which Western developments should provide a model for the rest of the world. But criticism of his work also highlighted the gap between scholars who stressed unevenness and complexity, as opposed to those who continued to push for some literally revolutionary transformation.

Disagreements were in part factual, of course. The gradualists argued that they had uncovered new data, particularly about sectors outside of product lines like cotton cloth. But the debate may also have reflected changes in conditions in the later twentieth century. Many historians who argued, like Rostow, for dramatic change grew up intellectually in the 1950s and 1960s, when European and American growth rates were quite high; optimism about current trends might influence the selection of measurements for the industrial past. In contrast many of the critics wrote, after the 1970s, during decades in which growth rates slowed, which may have helped point them to seek new levels of complexity in the past as well. History debates of this sort mix questions of fact with more subjective factors, which adds to the challenge of sorting out a "true" picture.

In part of course this particular discussion involved a familiar dilemma: is the glass half filled or half empty? Transformation did not happen in a single year or two, and not everything changed even in a half century. But if partial and uneven developments are added up, over the span of several decades and since we know that even limited changes would ultimately accumulate into larger and more extensive disruptions, the revolutionary glass might reasonably be seen as substantially filled. It's a question of deciding on the appropriate measurements and the time frame, admitting some clear complexities.

The factual debate has continued. Figure 2.1 shows growth estimates in one of the classic studies of the British Industrial Revolution, by Phyllis Deane, and more recent calculations by N.F.R. Crafts (who in fact revised downward his own estimates between 1985 and the 1990s).

Obviously, Crafts now sees a very modest growth not only in Gross Domestic Product but even in industrial output in the later eighteenth century, and a more-modest-than-expected pattern even in the first decades of the nineteenth century. Crafts similarly revises downward the calculation of productivity growth, seeing only 0.3 percent per year all the way from 1780 to 1860 even in the industrial sectors, and much less than this in agriculture and the crafts.

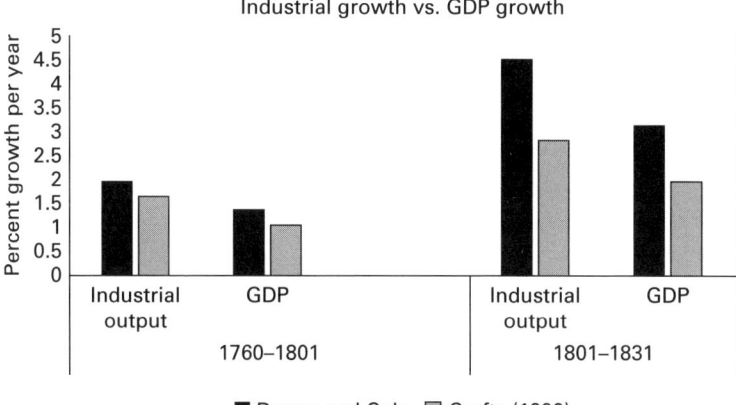

FIGURE 2.1 *From Harley, C.K. and N.F.R. Crafts, "Cotton Textiles and Industrial Output Growth during the Industrial Revolution,"* The Economic History Review, *48, No. 1 (1995): 134–44; Crafts, N.F.R and C.K. Harley, "Output Growth and the British Industrial Revolution,"* The Economic History Review, *45, No. 4 (1992): 703–30.*

See pp. 713–14 where Crafts and Harley explain their difference from Deane and Cole. Note that they did not uncover new data. The problem is that there are no really accurate figures for textile output in the eighteenth/early nineteenth centuries, and this was 40 percent of Britain's manufacturing total. Crafts and Harley simply recalculate, claiming Deane and Cole unreasonably inflated the cotton growth rate of expansion, to textiles in general. Why does debate center on the relative growth in cottons? Is this an important debate?

See, for the earlier data, Phyllis Deane and W.A. Cole, British Economic Growth, 1688–1959: trends and structure *(Cambridge: Cambridge University Press, 1962).*

Even with the ongoing discussions of quantitative data, the debate over whether there was an industrial revolution has died down considerably over the past 25 years. Some historians became more comfortable with the idea that an industrial revolution concept was still valid even though the whole process was less dramatic, more gradual than had earlier been thought. Additional data might help sort things out as well: one study emphasized the substantial growth of British exports, during the early nineteenth century, in the high-technology areas, which might seem to confirm genuine

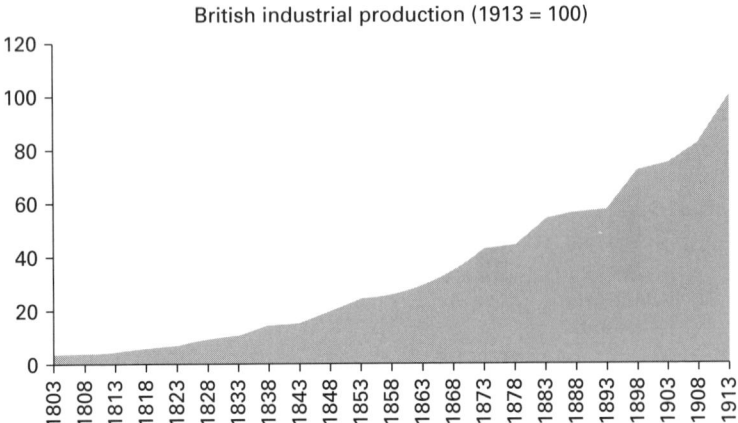

British industrial production (1913 = 100)

FIGURE 2.2 *From Crafts, N.F.R and C.K. Harley, "Output Growth and the British Industrial Revolution,"* The Economic History Review, *45, No. 4 (1992): 703–30.*

transformation and wide-ranging impact (not only in Britain, but in the societies where British goods were now out-competing local industry). Others, like Crafts himself, while downgrading the amount of measurable change in the early decades, took a longer view: by 1913, the accumulation of expansion would become undeniable, with a twentyfold growth in industrial production since 1803 (see Figure 2.2).

Even with renewed acceptance of the industrial revolution idea, however, enthusiasm for any simple model of change, along Rostow's lines, did not revive. The process was complex and prolonged, and these qualities would have to inform the effort to explain the causes of change as well.

One further component helped redirect analysis: the growing interest in comparing British (and Western) industrial patterns with the much different trajectory of economic development in other parts of the world during most of the nineteenth century. A global perspective raised huge new issues and causation—as we will see— but comparison tended to confirm that some sets of factors caused industrializing societies to "diverge" in massive ways from most other regions, and these factors had to be identified.

The human factor challenge: putting the people in

A further complication wrapped up in the basic definition of an industrial revolution involves what one might call the human face of the process and the ultimate impact of industrialization on key features of human life. Here too, there are important connections to the analysis of causation. The key criteria of industrialization risk seeming rather impersonal: growth of manufactured product, new types of machinery and energy sources. We will see that some of the explanations for industrialization focus—understandably enough—in accounting for these changes, without much attention to the people involved. And of course the interest in quantitative measurements of output or numbers of steam engines might detract as well from an understanding of the people involved, particularly when it seems that quantitative change was less massive than had previously been thought.

For it was true that in many ways the industrialization downplayed the human factor. Symbolically, a French textile manufacturer, in the 1830s, began rewarding the most productive machine each week by placing a bouquet of flowers on top (one assumes they wilted pretty quickly). In his industrial eyes, it was now equipment and not workers that deserved attention and credit. Capturing a similar shift in the balance between people and machines, a later author entitled his study of industrial society, "Mechanization Takes Command." We have also noted that a "great man" approach is not commonly used in identifying the causes of the industrial process, which were too complex and varied to be reduced to any individual genius.

But people, obviously, were deeply involved in all phases of industrial change, and arguably an explanation of why industrialization occurred must take relevant human motivations into account. Businessmen, if they were successful, could make a good bit of money from industrialization, in a few cases really substantial fortunes. But introducing novel equipment was a huge challenge— many early manufacturers did not know a lot about how the machines worked—and they had to invest what was for many of them substantial and risky amounts of money even to set up a small factory venture. And many failed: the success rate for new businesses in early industrialization was no more than 50 percent. Finally, at least at first, the calling of industrialist did not necessarily bring high prestige: many in the middle class continued to think that jobs in the State bureaucracy, or one of the established professions like law or medicine, or even merchant activities as opposed to the grubby job of manufacturing, carried more substantial status. So what would induce the pioneer industrialists and their early followers to do what they did? Causation here must carry over into possibly difficult individual decisions.

For the early industrialists were, of course, people, many of whom made really risky decisions. They might be greedy; they might be cruel to their workers (one spoke of how he had to "harden his heart" to his workers or he would not have been able to go on); but they worked quite hard for the most part, and they often knew that they were accomplishing something very new. A textile manufacturer in France, Motte-Bossut, who smuggled his machinery in from Britain in the 1820s, thus confronted his own parents, who ran a textile operation of their own employing manual workers. His parents were convinced that their son would fail and that his venture was really immoral—they resolutely refused to set foot in his growing factory—even when it was clearly proving to be a success.

Workers too faced huge challenges. Certain manufacturing jobs might have some advantages, but there is no question that factory life involved a faster pace and more intrusive supervision than more traditional work in craft shops or in the countryside. Here too, industrialization had a vital human face, and probably decisions that are even more difficult to explain than in the case of factory owners.

Many workers, crowded into slums in rapidly-growing cities, forced to walk considerable distances to work, faced genuine survival problems. At least in early British industrialization, health may have deteriorated. Certainly, with machines, there was much greater risk of accidents at work, and early employers often did not invest in basic safety equipment. While there were some skilled positions on the factory floor, most workers were semi-skilled, trained on the job, without much chance for advancement. Growing specialization of tasks made it hard for many workers to have much connection with any finished product, which might make it difficult to find any clear purpose in work.

But the biggest challenges, over time, were undoubtedly wrapped up in pace and supervision. Factories placed most workers under the control of foremen, rather than ever having the opportunity to make their own decisions about what to do on the job. Foremen might be nice, might be nasty, but the fact was that most factory hands were bossed around throughout their working lives. The pressure to work fast was obvious: the pace was set by machines, more than worker choice, and each generation of machines ran more rapidly than the last. And everything now ran according to clock time: workers were required to show up at a certain time (or lose wages and pay fines); they were usually locked in factories to prevent unexcused absences; and then, after 12 or more hours, the clocks finally let them go.

Obviously, many workers managed to adjust to these new work patterns, though they sometimes protested and more often simply took unauthorized time away from work to restore some sense of control. But there was strain. A German worker, for example, noted that his body shook after a workday: "my eyes burn so that I can hardly sleep."

The Industrial Revolution also challenged family life. Work was pulled away from home and family, as it moved into the factories. This forced decisions about who would stay home to care for children, and in many industrial revolutions new divisions opened up between men and women, at least for many decades. And what about the kids themselves? Many early factories employed child labor, partly to cut costs; and the results could be accidents, exhaustion, sexual abuse. Over time, however, machines became more complicated, and some of the tasks for children were automated. Social pressures created new laws limiting child labor and requiring schooling, and while these took time to gain full effect, ultimately the Industrial Revolution forced a redefinition of childhood, away from work and direct contributions to the family economy, and toward schooling and new levels of expense. Not surprisingly, again over time, the result was an unprecedentedly low birth rate. The Industrial Revolution, in other words, required basic changes at a very personal level.

The biggest human effects of the Industrial Revolution obviously bore on industrialists and factory workers. But other groups were touched. Craft workers, for example, worried about the threat of factory competition in any event, saw their employers putting pressure on them to produce more. Many rural women, who traditionally had produced thread or cloth by hand, were forced out of their jobs by machine-made goods; they had to decide between growing poverty or moving to cities where, often, the jobs most readily available were in domestic service or prostitution.

People were also affected by the Industrial Revolution as consumers. Opportunities and pressures to buy factory-made items increased. In the 1830s several Parisian businessmen organized the world's first department store, reflecting the need to find new ways to dispose of greater output. While the relationship between industrialization and consumerism is complicated, as we will see, there is no question that early industrialization pushed consumer roles to new levels. By the 1870s, to seize on a dramatic side-effect, doctors were studying a new illness: kleptomania, or a compulsion to steal goods one did not need.

On many levels, then, the barebones definition of industrialization must also encompass the wider human impacts of new machines and factories. For growing numbers of people, any industrial revolution forced substantial redefinitions of work, but also of life off the job and with family. The human effects link directly to questions about the causes of change: why would many people prove willing to accept the massive adjustments industrialization required? Or did they have any choice in the matter, given the weight of larger, impersonal factors? Particularly in Chapter 5, we will take up the issue of human motivations, but the theme bears on any aspect of the debates over causation.

The challenge of geography

Questions of where the Industrial Revolution occurred impinge even more directly on causation debates than do the issues of extended duration and the human side. The fact is that the Industrial Revolution can be considered a British phenomenon, a Western phenomenon, or a global phenomenon, with different chronologies attached to each option. Obviously, causation decisions differ considerably depending on which focus prevails. And to confuse the issue even more, some historians have not been terribly precise as to which spatial-temporal definition they are exploring. Some—not all—of the debate over industrial causation is a debate over what variant is being emphasized.

The British case

Without question, the only "pure" industrial revolution occurred in Britain, beginning in the mid-to-late eighteenth century. The development in Britain was, self-evidently, the only industrial revolution that did not have an established model to copy. We will see that, in some assessments of causation, foreign patterns did influence Britain too, but not in the direct sense of offering a full and explicit example of what industrialization was all about.

For some historians (not surprisingly, often British ones), explaining the British Industrial Revolution is the only analytical task worth tackling. They are either uninterested in explaining other industrial revolutions, or they assume that these simply arose naturally on the strength of the British example. National pride aside, it stands to reason that the causes involved in spurring the British process were the most urgent and elaborate, just as the question of timing is particularly complex. Motivations for innovation had to be particularly strong.

British industrialization featured many of the core inventions, including the steam engine—though important early industrial technologies did emerge elsewhere—in Western Europe and the United States. It was in Britain that the first whole industries, led by cotton spinning, were converted to factory production, even before the generalized application of steam. Britain led as well in railway development, a few decades after industrialization gained momentum, and was a pioneer as well in steam shipping. The first industrial working class, and the first group of identifiable industrialists, emerged in Britain. Finally, as we have seen, Britain was the first country to complete the basic industrialization process. By around 1850, not only was half of the population urban, but within the cities the factory working class in Britain had become as large as the craft worker population.

There is no question that any approach to industrial causation must foreground Britain, even if other cases are tackled as well. Why did industrialization first occur in Britain and not elsewhere? Why was the first outcropping an eighteenth-century development, rather than earlier or later? Questions of this sort, about time and place, are fundamental to causation analysis. Eighteenth-century Britain is the prime mover for industrialization.

The Western case

Beginning by the 1820s, a number of other societies began their own industrial revolutions. Belgium, France and the new United States were first in line, but Germany and some other regions in Western Europe soon followed. Obviously, this cluster of second-wave industrializations depended heavily on the British example. For businessmen, Britain provided an illustration of the feasibility but also the profit of the new forms of manufacturing. For governments, British prosperity was also attractive, but so were the military and diplomatic implications of industrial strength and technology. More than motivation was involved. Second-wave industrializations found some British businessmen locating in these new areas, bringing their knowledge with them. British factory workers also went abroad, helping to develop necessary skills for example in machine-building in return for bonus wages. British workers in France, highly paid, nevertheless claimed to suffer from the absence of good beer. Both foreign businessmen and skilled workers directly imported British machinery. British law made export illegal for several decades, in a futile attempt to protect trade secrets, but people copied designs on visits or even smuggled equipment out on boats.

Imitation, then, clearly figures into causation at this point, which is why some historians, preoccupied with the singular British achievement, begin and end their analysis with the British case. But at least two important causation issues attach to the West's industrial expansion, and they may be as interesting and significant as the "why Britain" challenge, or almost so.

First: why some Western countries and not others? What causes explain differential response within the West, for at least several decades? Why was the Netherlands, for example, so reluctant to change its economic patterns, compared to neighboring Belgium? The French response is even more widely discussed. France did industrialize, but slowly and long and incompletely, compared not only to Britain but also to Belgium and Germany—a lag that France would ultimately regret—as it contributed to growing military disadvantage vis-à-vis its German neighbors. What causes explain the German advantage, after centuries of considerable disarray; or explain the French hesitancy, after centuries of European leadership? Here is a specific kind of causation focus, but one that may shed light on the larger causation package for industrialization more generally. Another specific is obvious: why the United States (the first industrial case geographically removed from Europe)? What connections apply here?

And second: why the West, rather than other parts of the world or indeed the whole world? Why were so many Western nations able to industrialize more than half a century before any other part of the world? Granting a British lead, is it not more accurate to see industrialization as a Western phenomenon, more than a specifically British one? It is possible to suggest that, while Britain had a few specific features that explained its head start, it was ultimately a set of Western factors, in which Britain shared, that proved most decisive. (Indeed, if the French Revolution and Napoleonic Wars had not distracted neighboring European countries, industrialization might have arisen in other parts of the West even earlier.) What, then, is the most appropriate and significant geographic target for explanation? Whatever the attention to the British case, it is clear that the ability to imitate the British example was not automatic, otherwise more regions, including Muhammad Ali's Egypt, would have been involved. Causation analysis has to explain clear differentials in response to the British example, both within the West and between the West and other areas. Quite properly, a considerable portion of the most recent causation debates have ultimately revolved around filling these analytical gaps, rather than paying homage to Britain alone. Choosing relevant geography, perhaps even more than choosing relevant timing, is a key element in framing any realistic effort at explanation.

The idea of a Western focus, finally, embraces one other challenge: causation must explain not only why the West, but also, to the extent possible, why *not* other regions (including places like Egypt, which actually made the early effort but failed). Explaining why *nots*—why something did *not* happen, at least for a while—is harder even than explaining major innovations that did occur. In this case, there is the additional danger of facile potshots at the drawbacks of cultures or institutions outside the West, when the explanations are arguably far more complex. But there was a comparative difference, for several decades and often beyond, and many debates over causation have tried to account for this fact.

The global case

Industrial revolutions began to spread beyond the West by the end of the nineteenth century. By the 1880s, Japan launched a clear process that ultimately led to the creation of a powerful industrial economy. Russian industrialization also began around that point, though it would take on additional contours after the 1917 revolution and the advent of a communist regime.

A number of causation issues clearly arise from this global scope and the related idea of "latecomer" industrialization outside the West. Some of the issues directly connect to the analysis applicable to Britain and Western Europe, but some are new. Did societies that were not part of the Western tradition—and that were also geographically distant from pioneer Britain—need to find or to generate some special factors that would compensate for a different cultural or institutional framework? Or does a standard causation model, initially derived from the Western experience, continue to apply? Russian and Japanese industrializers had even more opportunities to imitate established players than countries like Germany and the United States had enjoyed. They could import more advanced machinery— copy more sophisticated factory forms—which is precisely what Russia and Japan did, as part of initiating their own process of change. To take one specific example, by 1914 half of all Russian industrial firms were owned by West Europeans, mainly Belgians, Germans, and French. On the other hand, "latecomers" faced some special disadvantages. Western competition was fierce, and it was hard to break through to full competitiveness. Established industrialization in some regions in many ways made it harder for later entrants, requiring additional and compensatory causation. It might take some special efforts to generate sufficient motivation and capacity to win through.

This is already an intriguing package. A global approach to industrialization, embracing major latecomer cases, requires decisions about what standard causes existed or had to be generated in order to prompt ongoing industrialization, using earlier assessment of the Western experience to guide this list. It also must explore distinctive factors, different from the earlier Western package that now worked into the mix. In general, latecomer industrializers saw a larger role for governments, which worked to provide, through State policies and encouragements, some of the causes that had operated more independently in the earlier Western cases.

And there is more. Even aside from the overall framework of latecomer industrializations, some specific questions apply to Japan and Russia. As with the West earlier—as with France or Germany— each regional case generates its own set of comparative causation issues; but now the stage is global.

Japan had not been an active participant in global trade before 1868. It was poor in relevant resources, including fuel sources, textile fibers other than silk (which was hard to industrialize fully), and some key metals. Adding to the burdens of industrialization, in other words, the country had to import far more resource components than was common. Some special causes must have been available to explain how the nation had both the motivation and the capacity to move forward.

Russia in some ways requires less special explanation. The country had many established ties to the West, and it was rich in basic resources. Yet it was a strongly agricultural economy, with relatively small cities, before industrialization began. And then under communism, when relationships with other parts of the world diminished and the new regime tried to spur industrialization on its own, there was a need to find some new ways to move the process to new levels. Again, some special causes and compensations were involved.

And finally, linked to the more specific analysis of Japanese and Russian factors, there is the comparative causation question: why these countries and not others? Most obviously, why Japan and not China, as Asia's first major industrializer? Analysis of this sort, but applying now to a later timeframe and a wider global mix, extends the assessment of reasons for industrialization but also reasons for its absence.

Another small but important batch of industrial revolutions developed in the 1950s and 1960s, particularly in the "Pacific Rim" countries like South Korea, Taiwan, and Singapore. Analyzing latecomer causation can usefully be extended to this new series as well, with some connection to explanations applied earlier to Japan.

The point is not to multiply regional examples endlessly. But each of the major waves of industrialization raises three kinds of causation questions, building on the evaluations previously applied to Britain and the West.

- First: what standard causes help explain industrialization wherever it took shape, from Britain onward?

- Second: what additional or special causes were added (besides imitation) in the major later cases, from Western Europe and the United States onward?

- Third: why, even by the 1960s, had industrialization taken firm hold only in several regions of the world, and not more generally? What factors seemed to divide industrializers from regions where industrial change occurred more slowly and haltingly?

Industrialization of the world

By the end of the twentieth century a process of ongoing industrialization began to embrace most of the world, and not just a few regions. By 2010 (when half of the world's population now lived in cities), about 60 percent of the world's population lived in societies that were either industrial or rapidly on the way to becoming so; in contrast, in 1900, only 20 percent had been involved. This was a huge shift in world history.

Global industrialization was a huge development, among other things cutting into regional economic inequalities that had widened earlier. In many ways, it reflected the fact that most societies had now developed the motivations and capacities that previously had applied to only a few, combined with growing opportunities to imitate established success stories. Causation analysis, by the same token, becomes less challenging, in some ways less essential, because so many regions had devised a successful formula. Still, there is an opportunity briefly to discuss how causes of change were beginning to be supplied more widely, and still, if again briefly, to note special factors in societies that were not fully engaged in change.

The Industrial Revolution was a genuine transformation in world history, even if its momentum built up over several decades. It changed human life, even some of the basic features of most individual families. It was a global development from the outset, but its unfolding was complicated, as only a few societies initially were able to participate directly. Far more felt the impact of competing factory imports or pressures to produce more foods and raw materials. Comparison, among the various societies that would ultimately join the industrial parade, remains essential. Transformation; human scale; global dimensions; here are three vital characteristics to keep in mind as we begin to probe how historians have tried to explain the reasons for such an upheaval.

For further discussion

(1) How significant are the revisions on British industrial growth rates, as established by recent studies? Do they challenge the idea of an industrial "revolution"?

(2) What are the key features of the Industrial Revolution? What were the main ways that industrial economies differed from previous economic patterns?

(3) Why were growth rates not faster during early industrialization?

(4) In what ways is an industrial revolution harder to define than a political revolution? Why has the industrial revolution concept prompted debate? What if anything turns out to have been revolutionary? What are the main disputes about basic data on industrial change?

(5) Is it better to define an industrial revolution through statistics or through qualitative human factors?

(6) What are the best ways to defend the validity of the industrial revolution concept? But also: what is an alternative way to look at changes and continuities during the same time period?

(7) How and why do current conditions influence historians' views of the past? Use discussions of industrialization to illustrate your assessment.

(8) How did the Industrial Revolution change family life?

(9) Why did many businessmen, as well as workers, see the Industrial Revolution as a source of stress?

(10) What are the issues in figuring out when and where the Industrial Revolution occurred?

Further reading

For accounts of the Industrial Revolution as revolution: T. H. Ashton, *The Industrial Revolution, 1760–1830* (Oxford: Oxford University Press, 1969); David Landes, *The Unbound Prometheus: Technological Change and Industrial Development in Western Europe from 1750 to the Present*, 2/e (Cambridge, UK: Cambridge University Press, 2003). See also Joel Mokyr, *The Lever of Riches: Technological Creativity and Economic Progress* (New York: Oxford University Press, 1990). The Rostow approach appears in W.W. Rostow, *The Stages of Economic Growth: A Non-Communist Manifesto*, 3/e (Cambridge, UK: Cambridge University Press, 1990). For debate, see Rondo Cameron, *A Concise Economic History of the World: From Paleolithic Times to the Present*, 4/e (New York: Oxford University Press, 2002); and N.F.R. Crafts, *British Economic Growth During the Industrial Revolution* (New York: Oxford University Press, 1986).

Debates are summarized and assessed in three useful articles: Peter Temin, "Two Views of the British Industrial Revolution," *The Journal of Economic History*, 57, no. 1 (March 1977); David Greasley and Les Oxley, "Endogenous Growth or 'Big Bang': Two Views of the First Industrial Revolution," *The Journal of Economic History*, 57, no. 4 (December 1977); and David Cannadine, "The Present and the Past in the English Industrial Revolution 1880–1890," *Past and Present*, no. 103 (May 1984). A recent presentation of N.F.R. Crafts' work is: C.K. Harley and N.F.R. Crafts, "Cotton Textiles and Industrial Output Growth during the Industrial Revolution," *Economic History Review*, 48 (1995): 134–44.

On global and social aspects of the Industrial Revolution, see Peter N. Stearns, *The Industrial Revolution in World History*, 4/e (Boulder, CO: Westview Press, 2013); and Jeff Horn, Leonard N. Rosenband, and Merritt Roe Smith (eds.), *Reconceptualizing the Industrial Revolution* (Cambridge, MA: Massachusetts Institute of Technology Press, 2010).

3

Initial explanations:

Working the Industrial Revolution into British and European history

This chapter sketches the history of early efforts to explain industrialization, and more generally to work the Industrial Revolution into serious historical coverage. The goal is to provide a baseline for understanding the more recent evolution of historical explanations and the emergence of more focused debates.

Early historical treatment directly raised three kinds of causation questions that set the stage for later analysis. First, was there a temptation to jump too readily at some explanations that might turn out to involve more correlation than cause? This might be an understandable confusion in getting started in analysis, but it also explains why more recent analysis had to change the focus considerably. Second, was the list of components adequate? Early treatments sought to identify possibly relevant ideas about policy; investment sources; labor sources; and developments in the transportation field. What did this list leave out? Did it generate a useful sense of prioritization among the core factors? And finally, inevitably, geography again: all the early treatments assumed that industrialization was a Western phenomenon, and some paid attention only to Britain. What were some early differences between a Western and a British approach, in looking for causes, and what limitations resulted from leaving out the rest of the world?

The Industrial Revolution entered quite gradually into standard historical coverage. The term itself was introduced into England by British intellectual Arnold Toynbee only in the 1880s (though German Marxists had identified it earlier). Even after that, however, most historians of Britain and modern Europe preferred to focus on political events and major wars and diplomatic alignments. After all, there was a lot to chew on in nineteenth-century history with the French Revolution and attendant reactions and wars, subsequent revolutions, nationalism and its diplomatic repercussions, and European imperialism, with the First World War as an ominous endpoint. There was even a long-standing bias against paying too much attention to the modern world at all, a sense that real historical precision and objectivity were possible only when directed toward more remote time periods.

In this general context, it was not surprising that initial causation analysis was not very explicit, and that it took some time for any sense of real debate to emerge. Greatest effort, even by economic historians who did register the importance of industrialization, went into placing the Industrial Revolution into a more standard narrative flow in British or European history, linking it to changes in government policy and economic theory primarily, with perhaps a bit of interest in explaining the heightened pace of technological innovation or invention. The factors that emerged from this narrative are still well worth considering, but they set a framework for more intensive debate rather than introducing debate directly. A few of the initial staples have been redefined as a result of more detailed research— the role of the English "enclosure movement" is a case in point—as we will see. Far more have been assigned a lower priority as causation debates have become more explicit. Part of any assessment of more recent discussions must however recognize the initial base, from treatments up to the middle decades of the twentieth century. This chapter summarizes the early efforts at explanation to provide a kind of baseline, allowing later chapters to explore changes but also continuities or recurrences in historical treatments.

Most standard accounts long placed their greatest emphasis on a description of changes, like the steady flow of new inventions or the creation of new factories and business forms; sections on causation were decidedly brief. Primary emphasis, understandably, sought to identify developments right before industrialization proper, from which the process might directly emerge. This is where the fairly familiar reliance on shifts in economic thought and government policy took pride of place, but it was supplemented by other factors. Quite properly, developments in the eighteenth century, from which British industrialization might directly emanate, received the most attention. On the whole, the standard picture involved a mix of several elements, operating in the same time period, from which the Industrial Revolution seemed to flow fairly smoothly. If by more recent standards the first approaches seem rather conventional, and certainly geographically parochial, at least they launched the process of analysis. Further, with some variations in specific emphases, they established a standard account that seemed acceptable for quite a while.

The long-accepted accounts did however raise a key question, which would later generate more explicit debate: were the factors directly connected to the actual process of industrialization, or were the connections just assumed because of coincidence in time? Was the research involved sufficiently careful in this regard? Chronological correlation, after all, is not the same thing as a cause and effect relationship. Explaining a general change like the Industrial Revolution almost inevitably produces challenges of this sort, where initial analysis makes assumptions that later research can then test more precisely.

A first cut: Toynbee's assessment

The initial effort to highlight the Industrial Revolution did include an explicit interest in causation, in what historian Arnold Toynbee called the "actual causes of economic development." Toynbee's essay spent surprisingly little time actually defining what he meant by industrial revolution: the main focus here was on the growth of cities, particularly factory cities, and of manufacturing products, along with attendant changes in agricultural productivity; new technologies won only passing mention. But on causes Toynbee was quite clear: the motive force involved the new economic ideas of Adam Smith and his three immediate economist successors, Thomas Malthus,

David Ricardo and John Stuart Mill. No other factors were really considered, though Toynbee was aware of additional developments like rapid population growth that would later be folded into historical explanations.

For Toynbee, what the new economic ideas did, in their focus on economic individualism, the profit motive and the importance of laissez-faire government policies, was displace a whole network of premodern rules, from land use to guild restrictions, that had inhibited innovation and the movement of labor: as Toynbee put it, "the essence of the Industrial Revolution is the substitution of competition for . . . medieval regulations." With new land policies, and particularly the opportunities provided by enclosure of small landholdings into large estates, rapid improvements could be introduced in farming and meat production. In manufacturing, with the end of guild rules and a larger commitment to free trade, the basic technological and organizational changes central to industrialization would easily follow. Toynbee spent some time on the downsides of early industrialization and the absence of protective regulations, but ultimately his was a story of progress. And it was a strictly British story: industrial revolutions elsewhere offered no interest in this account. Nor was there any real effort to show the specific links between new ideas and the actual processes of industrial change. Once competition was freed, and the government ended its support for old restrictions or provided frameworks, like land enclosure, that did the same job, a new economic system unfolded rather automatically.

Government policy and ideological change

Standard economic histories by the mid-twentieth century reflected some of the same emphases as Toynbee had suggested, including the power of new economic theory, but now in an expanded framework. Alterations in government policy, most notably, involved more than the new ideas, for there was also a commitment to promoting new infrastructure and other enhancements. Further, some of the accounts began to branch out from Britain alone, to some consideration of Western Europe more generally.

In this expanded approach, a key political shift began to take shape as early as the seventeenth century, through a growing sense of responsibility, on the part of government leaders, for economic growth, amid increasing diplomatic and military competition among the European states. At first, a doctrine of mercantilism prevailed, urging government support for new manufacturing ventures and other developments that would encourage greater trade and output. Mercantilist doctrines encouraged governments to reduce local tariffs and other internal barriers to trade, a major development in countries like France. This was part of the creation of more national, rather than local markets, and could clearly spur new levels of specialization and overall production. (Germany, though still divided among separate states, launched a similar effort in the early nineteenth century, in a national customs union, the *Zollverein*.) Mercantilist states also promoted attention to roads and canals, again to facilitate economic activity. Mercantilism embraced two limitations, however, that had to be addressed before full industrialization could emerge. First, mercantilists tied economic policies closely to military competition and colonial advancement, even believing that gains by one state would necessarily lead to losses by another: there was no way to grow the whole economic product, merely to re-divide it through national rivalries. Second, while mercantilist officials might want to promote growth, they also used the government to regulate economic operations, often trying to protect existing methods against too much innovation.

Government economic sponsorship unquestionably continued in the eighteenth century. The British government undertook a substantial program of canal building and road paving. Some military motives contributed here, toward easier movement of troops to quell protest or protect against invasion, but the main goal was economic growth. Indeed, the new routes did facilitate the movement of foods and manufactured products. They could also help new industrialists combine coal resources with supplies of iron, a vital blend in early industrialization; canals, supplementing river ways and coastal routes, were particularly important here. In all later industrializations, from Western Europe and the United States onward, the Industrial Revolution would also follow from at least the early stages of railway and steamship development, which even more clearly than British waterways improvements spurred the flow of goods. But later cases could also reveal the limitations of transportation gains, in countries where a new infrastructure led to more raw materials and food exports but not to an industrialization process. Transportation gains turned out to be an essential but not sufficient element in explaining industrial revolutions, and in defining the role of governments in spurring change.

In addition to the transportation issue, government action was also essential in introducing greater order into banking systems. Gradually, during the eighteenth century, with government encouragement, the Bank of England emerged as a central agency, reducing a welter of competing operations and sometimes irresponsible investment schemes. The new banking system did not involve itself directly in the newer kinds of industries; investment funds came from less formal and more scattered sources, with factory industry long seeming too risky for the most established financiers. But in the standard accounts, banking stabilization was another government contribution to the framework from which industrialization would emerge.

At the same time, however, government approaches also had to change, to move away from pure mercantilism, even as the State's role in transportation and banking stabilization continued to expand. Removing mercantilist interference with economic activities and technologies was at least as important, so the standard argument ran, as the State's new role in transportation and banking. Indeed, from the middle of the eighteenth century a number of economists— benefitting from the growing attention the European Enlightenment encouraged to what we now call the social sciences—began to question mercantilist assumptions about the limits to overall economic growth and the need for detailed State oversight. But it was the 1776 publication of the *Wealth of Nations*, by the Scottish philosopher and economist Adam Smith that really signaled a fundamental change. Here is where the focus on the State combined with arguments about the power of new ideas.

For as Arnold Toynbee had already highlighted, Adam Smith, ushering in what came to be known as the liberal or laissez-faire school of economics, argued that unfettered private competition, not government action, was the soundest path for economic growth and overall prosperity. Individual profit motives were the best spur to positive change, and while they might be selfish they would combine, through competition, to promote the lowest possible prices and highest quality; it was as if an "invisible hand" assured the general good from the welter of individual strivings. Smith was followed by many other economists, into the nineteenth century and beyond, who urged elimination of needless internal economic regulations and also, usually, the abolition of tariffs on international trade, all in the name of maximal economic growth.

Under this spur, British and European governments did begin to relax some of their oversight efforts, for example pulling back from any attempt to limit the introduction of new technologies. And while actual policy change was gradual and a full "laissez-faire" or hands-off approach never entirely prevailed, the chronological coincidence between the new ideas, and Smith's publication specifically, and the initial stages of real industrialization certainly makes a positive connection highly plausible. New economic thinking, applied to governments already interested in economic growth, may have set the scene for the inventors and entrepreneurs who actually did the work of the early industrial revolution.

Even with this connection, however, government withdrawal remained only part of the story. It continued to be essential for governments to maintain an active role in some aspects of the economy. Protection of merchants abroad was a vital function, as trade increased with early industrialization; this included increasingly vigorous efforts against piracy. Transportation oversight was another core area. Government promotion of roads and canals was soon combined with encouragement for railway development. In Britain, private companies did most of the direct railway work, but they operated with government sponsorship and particularly the government's right of eminent domain, which allowed seizure of land for the new train routes. And outside of Britain, the State's role in railway development was considerably more elaborate, as in the gifts of vast tracts of public land the United States government provided to railroad developers to help motivate the whole effort. Finally, though this was often at most a footnote in the early explanations of industrialization, all early industrial governments used police and armies to put down labor risings, making it clear, through the initial industrial decades at least, that strikes and unions were illegal.

The State's role in early industrialization was thus complex. Nevertheless, it was long easy to argue that a variety of changes in State activities, including but not confined to the new approaches urged by the liberal economists, provided a vital backdrop for the Industrial Revolution. In turn, industrialization fitted neatly into historians' focus on the political sphere as the principal component of standard historical narratives.

Finally, the political approach also helped explain comparisons between British and continental European patterns, as this kind of analysis extended through further historical treatments of industrialization. What the British government did spontaneously or under the guidance of the new economists, continental governments would begin to undertake only after assimilating key results of the French Revolution of 1789 and its impact on adjacent countries. Though there are many disputes over specifics, the French Revolution did broadly advance middle-class interests as against those of the aristocracy, in ways that were soon relevant to industrialization. It also, more specifically, eliminated remaining manorial restrictions on the movement of rural labor, in abolishing serfdom; and a key law, the LeChapelier law of 1791, abolished the craft guilds, which could open the way for the introduction of new technologies and methods as against longstanding regulations which sought to maintain established procedures. The revolution also completed the process of eliminating regional barriers to national trade. All of this might seem to confirm the importance of political change in setting the stage for industrialization, even though Britain provided the essentials earlier, and on a different basis, from its continental neighbors.

Resources and labor

None of the standard accounts rested on State action, or inaction, alone. Some attention to available natural resources was essential, though as we will see this subject raises some immediate complexities in causation analysis. Most coverage also sought to explain where the initial factory workforce might come from, though the assessment seldom commanded much detail.

Early industrial revolutions, beginning with Britain's, required access to coal: here was the fuel that powered the steam engines, and it was heavy to move. A supply of iron was vital as well, and as charcoal smelting declined, the capacity to move iron ore to the sources of coal, or vice versa, was crucial. Early industrialization depended, finally, on relevant supplies of textile fibers, and particularly cotton, which proved most easily mechanized and which steadily gained in popularity among consumers.

Britain had advantages in all these resource areas. Its substantial holdings in coal were also, often, located near waterways or were directly adjacent to deposits of iron ore. Britain also learned early—among European countries generally—about cotton from its dealings with India, and then developed an important additional supply with the expansion of cotton production in the American South.

There are some important logical challenges, however, in moving too quickly from resource analysis to an explanation of industrialization. Basic resources like iron and steel, as in the British case, cannot by themselves cause industrialization, for the simple reason that they were not novel factors. They had not newly relocated in the eighteenth century; their presence for millennia had not previously motivated fundamental change. To be sure, new transportation opportunities enhanced the opportunities to combine them to a modest degree. And British access to cotton was genuinely improving, though the question of assuring adequate supply warranted recurrent attention. Overall, however, resources helped facilitate industrialization once other factors set the process in motion; by the same token absence of resources might explain why an industrial revolution did NOT occur. Only recently, as we will see in the following chapters, has a more sophisticated argument worked resources more directly into the fundamental eighteenth-century pattern of change.

One particular British development, however, further involves the resource equation. It came up both in early explanations and, as we will see later on, in a somewhat different and more precise form later on. Many economic historians seized on reports of a decline in wood supply in Britain, by the early eighteenth century, affecting fuel for heating and for manufacturing alike, including of course the use of charcoal for smelting iron. Growing population and rising economic activity strained Britain's timber resources. As a result, aristocratic landowners and eager businessmen alike sought to expand Britain's coal output in compensation; and of course they could take advantage of the abundant resources available, sometimes located on aristocratic estates. Expansion of coal production, in turn, called forth other innovations, such as the initial steam engine, invented in 1712 to help pump water from coal mines as shafts were driven deeply in order to increase output; and the replacement of charcoal encouraged other innovations in iron production directly. While the first steam engine— the Newcomen engine—had no other uses, it obviously set a precedent that could be taken up a few decades later when the goal was activation of a wider range of manufacturing equipment. Changes in wood supply, in sum, prodded a new British interest in exploiting coal, with other changes gradually ensuing in consequence. Here then is a factor different from resource availability overall, which conceivably helps explain the timing of change and may well provide one of the key reasons a process was set in motion with Britain uniquely in the lead.

The question of labor, though it characteristically received less attention than the issue of natural resources, offered a different set of causation issues. There is no question that a growing number of workers had to be drawn into factory industry for industrialization to take off. This new working class was initially limited—again, industrialization started small—but it expanded very rapidly in relationship to the overall population. Early histories of the Industrial Revolution, if they considered workers at all, did not probe too deeply—asking for example whether workers were drawn to factories or rather had to be prodded into them—but there was some awareness of the availability issue.

And here, as with wood supply, historians quickly uncovered a plausible new eighteenth-century element, fairly distinctive to Britain: the growing enclosure movement. During the middle decades of the century, many landowners, seeking to develop larger holdings for exploitation in commercial agriculture, persuaded the British parliament to pass acts of enclosure, requiring that owners in a particular area enclose their property with hedges. Small-holders could not usually afford this expense, which would additionally cut into the land available for agriculture. Many were forced to sell out to larger estates in the region. The results were: obvious consolidation of landholdings in many regions; new opportunities to grow crops or raise livestock for sale in urban markets (itself a crucial backdrop to industrialization, which required an expanding food supply); and new limits on opportunities for work in the countryside. Former peasant farmers, the argument went, were no longer needed in traditional numbers, because the new estates were more efficient. Thus they had no choice but to seek alternative support, mainly by flocking to early industrial cities and hoping they could find work, however unpleasant, in the pioneering factories.

This initial version of the enclosure explanation was later corrected, or even rejected, as we will see. But it did have the merit of seeing labor supply as an issue (and not some automatic response to whatever early factory owners decided to do) and of seeking a factor that would explicitly apply to the question of time and place—in later eighteenth-century Britain.

Capital

Investment funding was essential to get the early factories off the ground. By our standards, of course, the initial steam engines and other equipment were quite modest and relatively inexpensive. Factories might be installed in buildings initially constructed for other purposes, like convents or warehouses, which further reduced cost. But the fact was that some funding was essential, and in a few cases like some of the larger iron works or, later, the establishment of rail lines, the investment requirements were considerable. This means in turn that any explanation of what caused the Industrial Revolution has to come to grips with the sources of the capital required.

Initial historians of early industrialization could point to a few aristocrats or other established families, of obvious means, who took an early role. This could include some of the landowners who sponsored the growing coal mines. In these cases, capital requires no special attention, for there was ample family money at hand. The question here might be less capital supply and more individual motivation: why would already wealthy individuals be interested in the newer ventures?

But the historians concerned with these issues realized that not all the pioneering factory owners came from established wealth.

Knowledge about origins was not initially extensive, and we will see that later discoveries contributed significantly to more sophisticated causation debates. But even early on it was clear that family wealth was not the only answer.

Many historians pointed to the growth of merchant activity during the century or so preceding industrialization, with far flung trade with the Americas and Asia. The Atlantic slave trade also brought profits back home to Britain and other countries in Western Europe. In broad outline, then, the initial industrial histories could be fairly confident on the capital side: overall sources were clear, and expansion during the decades before the Industrial Revolution began made perfect sense in terms of timing. Some histories tied in the improvements in banking to the capital discussions, adding to the understanding of how and when the investment could be accounted for.

As with labor, some of these initial explanations, though not entirely inaccurate, proved unduly general. They did not account for the difficulty many earlier factory owners actually faced in arranging for investment funds, or the pressures that resulted. References to rising trade or the banking system could well be too general—not wrong—but not fully applicable to the actual patterns of industrialization. But it would require additional research, and additional critical assessment, before these problems gained wide realization. For a time, availability of new capital seemed to fit fairly neatly with the other factors commonly cited in explaining why industrialization, and why in eighteenth-century Britain.

Other elements—and some gaps

Initial efforts to explain industrialization did not systematically grapple with several facets of the process that would loom larger in later discussions. Explanation for the expanding rate of invention, for example, did not draw wide attention. There were some references to the importance of "artisan tinkerers", particularly in Britain. Many early inventors were in fact craftsmen who proved to have some genius in devising and applying innovation to the production process. Was this an accident? Was it, as some argued, the result of fairly loose guild traditions in Britain, which placed fewer constraints on seeking out new methods? The question was identified but not systematically pursued.

Pioneering businessmen comprised another category where motivations might be explored: why were some now willing to push out in new directions and why particularly in Britain? Again the issue was identified but not systematically probed. Some accounts did note that British aristocrats were more tolerant of business than their continental counterparts; a few even dabbled directly. This might generate an atmosphere of greater acceptance for new types of business ventures.

And what, finally, to posit concerning markets for new goods? This is a topic in itself, and part of a more general motivational context. Were there clear developments in potential markets for increased output that could help explain why inventors decided it was worth inventing, investors why it was worth investing, entrepreneurs why industrial innovation was worth the effort and risk? On the whole, early explanations of the Industrial Revolution focused much more clearly on supply issues—as with capital—or on issues of context—as with more government encouragement to competition—than on the demand side. Historians tended to assume that, in a still largely agricultural economy, increased production of manufactured goods would find ready sales, particularly since industrial technology tended to drive down prices because of greater labor efficiencies. Only later in industrialization, a common argument ran, when more sophisticated technologies and factories increased output still further, did industrialists have to worry explicitly about generating new markets. The argument here was not entirely wrong. The big expansion of sales forces and the generation of new types of advertising did await the 1830s and beyond. Nevertheless, the assumption that the market aspect of initial industrialization warranted no special attention turned out to be questionable; another area where first explanations—though important and plausible—would ultimately generate debate.

The expansion of industrialization

Many early histories of the Industrial Revolution focused on Britain alone. Exploration of factors like the enclosure movement followed from the need to explain Britain particularly, and could encourage a strictly British focus in turn. But some accounts went on to deal at least briefly with the initial phase of industrial expansion, particularly to other parts of Western Europe. Many of them found that they could readily apply many of the general categories of causation they had posited for Britain, but with different specific mechanisms and always, of course, with the additional element of imitation adding to the mix.

Government patterns thus were broadly similar, particularly after the impact of the French Revolution and attendant reforms elsewhere. Governments supported transportation improvements, but pulled back from detailed industrial regulation. As in Britain, they tried to protect factory owners from unions and labor protest. At the same time, their policies were strongly influenced by liberal economists, who picked up the banners of Adam Smith and his British successors in arguing for the benefits of business competition. Theorists like Jean-Baptiste Say, in France, or Frederick List in Germany replicated and extended British arguments about the importance of free enterprise. Continental governments hesitated, however, over the issue of lowering tariffs, believing that infant industries needed some protection, most obviously from British competition. And governments did on the whole play a somewhat more active role than the British model suggested, using government power to supplement private initiative in several areas to help set the process in motion as the British example commanded growing attention.

Capital, for example, remained an essential factor, and Western Europe benefited in general from some of the same international market expansion that had fed British coffers. The expansion of banking was a source of funds on the continent as well, and indeed explicit investment banks rose more quickly than had been the case across the Channel. But continental governments supplemented the capital formation process, providing more direct investment in areas like railroad development or, as in Prussia, building the system outright, on the basis of tax revenues. Inventions were vital, and French and other artisans contributed several key developments, most obviously in textiles; one French craftsman, for example, built a loom suitable for silk weaving with an automated panel that much later would serve as a prototype for computer technology. But imitation of Britain was an additional essential for the newer technologies as well, and governments, sponsoring technology fairs, worked hard on this angle along with enterprising businessmen. Finally, British industrialists, establishing operations in France or Belgium, directly imported both capital and technology; again providing standard factors in industrial development but in ways that differed from the original British model.

Labor supply is another consideration, introduced in the British case but carried over into explorations of continental industrialization. Skilled labor was partly, initially, provided by British migrants. The basic supply of workers, however, depended on influx from the countryside. While there was no enclosure movement, the end of serfdom and other changes in agriculture help explain additional if often reluctant availability.

Several continental countries had resources in coal and iron that were similar to the British case, again as facilitators rather than basic causes of change. But while there was no dramatic spur like the decline in wood supply, the desire to follow the British example provided its own new motivation for exploiting longstanding reserves. Further, since much continental industrialization was quickly associated with railroad development, which both required iron and coal supplies and provided additional methods of transportation, there was another basis for motivating resource use that matched the British process, albeit with different specifics.

Initial explanations of continental industrialization, then, could take advantage of factors identified in Britain while addressing the importance of imitation and exploring how different sources of innovation accounted for comparable basic factors. Continental developments were slowed by the period of the Napoleonic wars, which delayed full attention to the industrialization process. This aside, however, there was no initial sense that a dramatically distinctive causation model was required.

The demand side of the causation equation, finally, received no more attention in the initial probes of industrial expansion than had been the case for Britain. Continental countries—many government leaders, certainly many aspiring businessmen—began to seek an industrial revolution because of British success. As we have seen, military motives joined a quest for profit in spurring change. Historians and contemporaries alike may have assumed that new levels of output would find ready sales, and indeed the quick expansion of railroad systems generated an immediate market for heavy industrial goods that had taken longer to develop in Britain. As with the analysis of the British case, it would take some time for explanations of industrial expansion to venture a more subtle assessment of the motivational side of early industrial experience.

A number of economic historians contributed to the initial list of factors leading to industrialization. Emphases varied somewhat, but there were few major differences in the agenda, and scant direct debate. The initial approaches to causation at least provided a clear baseline—from which other questions and challenges could emerge—which in fact is what has happened in historical analysis over the past half-century.

Standard accounts clearly reproduced a plausible list of factors that had to be available for industrialization: infrastructure; suitable government policies and relevant economic ideas; available capital, raw materials, and labor. They had quite properly focused on the need to explain change: thus developments like wood supply, economic theory, or enclosure that helped explain eighteenth-century origins gained pride of place. Extension of analysis to Western Europe clearly developed a comparable checklist of factors, always with the opportunity and motivation of imitating Britain added in.

Despite frequent repetition in many standard European or British economic histories, the conventional causation package ultimately invited a number of debates, some of which remain quite lively today.

- There was the question, first, of moving away from coincidence in time to a more detailed investigation that would both check for accuracy—the enclosure explanation was an early target here—and also test direct connections to the actual industrialization process. Critical analysis was essential in this process, moving away from a largely descriptive approach.

- Comprehensiveness offered another test. We have already noted the absence of much attention to demand, or the markets for new levels of industrial production, where causation options were not initially clearly identified.

Motivation was also largely untreated, except insofar as new economic ideas might explain reasons to change behaviors. The standard causation analysis did not do a lot with the human element in industrialization, except perhaps in noting a special role for pioneering economic theorists.

- Prioritization was another challenge. The factors in the conventional analysis were plausible, and any discussion of causation must take them into account. But they were often presented without any particular effort to assess whether some were more important than others, and the attempt to fit them into a recognizable picture of European history tended to reduce any sense of real dynamism. Ultimately it became essential to juxtapose the list of standard factors with the sheer scope, the dramatic innovation, of the Industrial Revolution itself. Could a list of valid but individually fairly limited factors account for the sweeping change?

- Finally of course there was the unaddressed issue of geography. The conventional focus was entirely Western, chronologically confined to the later eighteenth/early nineteenth centuries. What would happen to the standard list if a more global framework was in play, with comparative questions also addressed back to the British/ Western inception point?

Questions of this sort would not emerge immediately. By the 1960s and 1970s, however, a new set of historians, though respectful of the standard account, began to raise the types of issues that would actually spark wider debate.

For further discussion

(1) Why was a focus on economic theory initially so attractive in explaining industrialization?
(2) Do all the components of the conventional picture of the factors leading to industrialization seem equally plausible? Are some

more important than others? What kinds of additional research and analysis would be most useful in testing and improving this standard account?

(3) Does the conventional list adequately explain why Britain industrialized first? Which factors most explicitly attach to Britain and to its launch in the eighteenth century? Can the same list be used to explain why other parts of Western Europe, plus the United States, joined in the process relatively quickly, in contrast to other world regions?

(4) And for speculation: what would a country like Japan, turning to industrialization only late in the nineteenth century, have to do to replicate the necessary causation for an industrial revolution? How much do opportunities for imitating successful industrial conversions in other societies reduce the need for independent causes of change?

(5) Finally: does the list of causes described so far account for the *magnitude* of industrial change, or is magnitude the appropriate target for analysis?

Further reading

See Arnold Toynbee, *The Industrial Revolution* (Devon, England: David & Charles, 1969).

For standard mid-twentieth-century accounts, see Witt Bowden, Michael Karpovitch, and Abbott Payson Usher, *An Economic History of Europe Since 1750* (Whitefish, MT: Literary Licensing, LLC, 2012); Phyllis Deane, *The First Industrial Revolution* (London, 1965); and W.O. Henderson, *Industrial Revolution on the Continent: Germany, France, Russia 1800–1914* (London: Routledge, 1961).

4

Why Britain?

Any causation discussion must include the question of why Britain so clearly took the lead in industrialization, at least three decades before any other society launched a process and as literally the only instance in which this kind of change occurred without the benefit of any external model. This is not the only causation question to ask, as we have seen, but it is certainly high on the list.

Early explanations of the Industrial Revolution were not always explicit about the British precedent. For many historians, including Toynbee, Britain was the only case worth mentioning, which meant that they focused on potentially British factors but without direct comparative analysis. Toynbee's insistence on the importance of the great economists resulted in an exclusively British list, but as we have seen there were similar theorists operating in several Western societies, if not quite as early as Adam Smith, at least soon thereafter. Economic theory might, in other words, help explain the British lead but Toynbee's exploration was not directly aimed at proving the point.

More broadly, the conventional explanations discussed in the previous chapter similarly fit Britain—and might be used to highlight its leadership—as in the emphasis on the enclosure movement, which was unquestionably a strictly British phenomenon. Some of the relevant analysis, however, also required additional work to address the British experience explicitly. Further complicating the picture was a natural process of reexamining key elements of the standard account. Detailed research raised important empirical issues with some of the elements involved, sometimes downgrading the importance of factors that had been previously highlighted.

Additional analysis also, however, identified several new factors that had previously been left out.

This chapter addresses the question of "why Britain?" first by picking up on some of the debates that took shape over the standard account and how they began to improve the focus on the comparative problems involved, particularly around banking or the role of the economists. We turn then to some of the newer elements that have been added to the assessment, around industrial demand but also the role of politics.

Debate over the British lead is ongoing, and an important recent work returns forcefully to the question, with some striking results. We conclude the chapter with this indication of the current status of this aspect of the larger causation debates. Britain will emerge again in later chapters, as a more global focus generated still further questions about the reasons for its special role. We must also return to the question about the relationship between the British precedent and later industrializations, in preparation for moving out on this broader facet of historical analysis.

Reviewing the standard list

Specific references to innovations in banking as a significant factor in Britain's industrial lead have declined dramatically. Unquestionably, capital was necessary for industrial investment. But we have seen that most early factory owners did not turn to banks for investment funds, relying rather on family money or individual partnerships. And of course early factories were mostly fairly small, which limited the initial investment needs. Furthermore, and this is the most important *new* finding, though Britain did introduce changes in banking during the eighteenth century, it is not clear that its banking structure was in any way superior to that available in other European countries. Some historians may understandably have confused the importance of investment banking in their own, more advanced industrial societies for the situation at the outset.

Even more striking, in terms of the long-accepted list of factors, is the effective disappearance of the role of the new economic theorists. Most critical accounts dealing with causation no longer even bring them up. This is not to say that they have disappeared from history: the economic theories were new (no debate there), and they have played a great part in the ongoing role of economics as a discipline and ultimately in its interactions with the policy world. Economists actively discuss the importance of free market policies in the world today, but of course that may be a separate issue from the question of initial industrial causation.

Adam Smith probably had little to do with early British industrialization. If anything his work reflected intelligent recognition of some of the economic changes that were occurring around him, such as greater specialization of labor in the burgeoning factories, than the other way around. The long identification of changes in theory with the emergence of industrialization was not based on careful inquiry into actual links with initial technologies and organizations, and confused coincidence in time with causation.

Most obviously, by the time Adam Smith wrote (in 1776) early British industrialization was already taking shape. Even if his ideas had gained a quick impact on policy—which was not fully the case— the connection simply emerges too late to play a major causal role. A role in *enhancing* industrialization later on, quite possibly; a role in changing economic policies in other countries, like Germany, in ways that might promote industrialization there is also worth considering. But this angle on the question of why Britain was first seems to have been a dead end.

Institutions and government

If elements of the conventional picture have been downgraded, much more attention has gone to laws and institutions as a key explanation for the British lead. There is no question that Britain experienced significant political changes about a century before the clear onset of the Industrial Revolution, and some of these changes set up a political structure that was different from most of its counterparts elsewhere in Europe, or the world. Exploring connections between political distinctiveness and industrial distinctiveness is clearly warranted. Further, in contrast to the situation with the new economic theorists, the chronology is suggestive as well: political change comes first, is digested and implemented over several decades, and then decisive economic change sets in, or at least so the argument could run.

The key political shift, completed through the Glorious Revolution of 1688, was the installation of a parliamentary monarchy, with fairly clear limits on royal power and considerable protection of various liberties, including freedom of religion for Protestants. Greater political stability resulted—and surely that was a valuable precondition for economic development, though not a direct cause. The more liberal climate may have encouraged an atmosphere of innovation, but it is hard to make direct connections with new technologies or organizational structures. Still, a leading economic historian (and Nobel Prize winner) Douglass C. North explicitly argued that "economic liberty, religious freedom, and representative government became intertwined issues," and the combination, he believes, was crucial to economic growth.

The British system did involve some clear limits on the authority of the central government, and some historians have highlighted this as a key element in the context for industrialization, extending the arguments about the importance of various freedoms. They particularly contrast this structure with more centralized regimes such as China. Businessmen, according to this approach, were freer to make decisions than their counterparts in many other societies, and they had fewer worries about arbitrary government interventions, and less uncertainty, as a result.

The institutional argument also emphasizes the importance of clear property rights, including new levels of protection for inventors through changes in the patent law during the seventeenth century. On the issue of rights in general, it was revealing that John Locke, the political theorist most closely associated with the Glorious Revolution, argued that property was a "natural right," along with life and liberty. Specific new protections for patented inventions might have been even more important (though we'll see that this angle has encountered some problems as well). North—again—argues directly that "England had begun to protect private property in knowledge with its patent law. The stage was now set for the industrial revolution."

Many economists continue to contend that a stable institutional context, including clear-cut commercial laws and assurance against arbitrary interventions, is an essential framework for economic development: this is an element still emphasized in explaining why some societies move more quickly than others toward industrialization even today. North's overall thinking has contributed greatly to this line of analysis. And in this sense, British institutions may indeed have been relevant to the nation's leadership in early industrialization. But there have also been a number of objections to the British institutional argument. Several historians have recently argued that it is very difficult to go from general British political patterns, such as the emergence of parliamentary power, and the actual technological changes that ushered in industrialization. They note that the Netherlands, which featured very similar political developments including religious freedom, in fact long lagged in industrial development. And they argue that claims about some special British interest in property rights is overblown, that property was in fact more clearly protected in other legal systems (such as the French, or even the Chinese). Here, clearly, is a significant and continuing debate over the kind of causation applicable to the question of "why Britain?"

The institutional approach may face one final challenge, though logically this is not connected to Britain directly. By 2012, indeed well before, it became clear that very different kinds of political regimes can generate industrial revolutions. Some stability and a clear legal system may be desirable, but personal freedoms, even clear titles to private property, are not always involved. This does not mean that the institutional approach to Britain itself is wrong, but it does encourage some additional questions.

Yet attention to a British policy angle continues. Patrick O'Brien has recently argued for the centrality of the State in Britain's industrial lead, but with some major new twists. He, too, emphasizes the role of stability; he argues in fact that even before the Glorious Revolution the nation's elite had decided that the State should provide a framework for economic growth, with particular attention to protecting commercial interests overseas. While the commitment of the State to protect the economy was a vital general element, O'Brien contends that it was taxation policy, combined with colonial holdings, that established a more specific spur. Firmer tax policies, which among other things took advantage of colonial expansion, allowed the government to protect economic security and property rights, but also invest in the domestic economy and subsidize the nation's global trade particularly through the large standing navy. O'Brien argues that no other state, at least in Europe, had these assets; some had colonial wealth, but their tax systems were far less efficient and their levels of internal stability, including protection from invasion, far less advanced. Britain alone had the political institutions that could really generate systematic profits from the colonial enterprise. Finally, Britain's reliance primarily on indirect taxes on property and goods (in contrast to direct payments as in France), gained acceptance for relatively high rates; and the taxes were collected by "one of the most professional and efficient bureaucracies" in Europe. Not only O'Brien, but also William Ashworth, contend that particular features of British taxation, as well as the resultant revenues, played a key role in ultimate industrialization; Ashworth sees tax policies, bent on helping Britain rival the initially larger but more traditional French economy, as crucial in allowing the state to oversee industrial development on a national scale.

Arguments of this sort, based mainly on fairly recent research, obviously call attention to some unexpected aspects of the larger argument concerning policy causation. Familiar elements, around British political stability, are supplemented by the claims about a larger and earlier state commitment to economic growth and particularly by the emphasis on tax systems and revenues, and the government's use of fiscal resources to fund instruments for expanding trade and manufacture. The State has returned, front and center, to the ongoing debate over "why Britain?"

Resources and labor

Other current explanations of British industrialization focus strongly on two different factors, however: labor costs and energy supplies and costs. Elements of this approach have long been discussed; as with the State, recent analysis mixes older and newer elements. But a number of economic historians have brought new energy to the discussion, along with a growing amount of precise quantitative data. And many of them focus so resolutely on their claims that they leave the State out altogether.

We have already noted that Britain enjoyed abundant supplies of coal. This was not new, of course, but it began to gain new importance during the seventeenth century because of the rising cost of wood. British forests began to be depleted at a fairly rapid rate, thanks to the use of wood in shipbuilding in addition to relying on wood for heating and (when converted to charcoal) in metallurgy. This situation provided clear motivation for a growing interest in coal as an energy source. Conversion was not automatic; a number of changes in technology were essential in order to use coal in manufacturing, and additional technological change, including the invention of the Newcomen engine to facilitate pumping water from deeper mine shafts, facilitated access to coal itself. The key point, following from the rising costs of traditional fuel, was that coal resources kept the prices of this energy source quite low. This became one of the two key ingredients for Britain's pioneering industrial role.

But this factor combined with relatively high wages. Over time, but well before industrialization proper, Britain had steadily expanded its manufacturing and commercial activities, which created a strong demand for workers. At the same time, particularly in the seventeenth century itself, the population remained relatively stable. Britain participated in a distinctive European family system that emphasized late marriage for most people, which helped curb birth rates compared to most other agricultural societies. In the British case, this population structure combined with the growing need for workers to create a distinctive wage structure. This structure, in turn, provided ample motivation for manufacturers to seek wage-saving technological changes.

Industrial technology, thus, responded to two vigorous trends by the late seventeenth and early eighteenth centuries, both of which clearly spurred innovation. Ultimately, during the eighteenth century itself, the two responses would marry, as the use of coal through the steam engine began to be combined with the inventions, like the flying shuttle, that interceded to reduce labor costs in manufacturing.

Only Britain, the argument concludes, had this distinctive combination. Other societies had ample coal reserves, but they did not face the same kind of shortage in wood-based fuels and they did not offer the high-wage economies that would spur this aspect of technological change.

No other explanation seems necessary, according to this powerful recent argument. Institutions might provide an encouraging context, but not direct causation. Favorable cultures can be considered, but again their link to actual technological development is loose at best. Human motivations are covered because people—inventors and entrepreneurs particularly—were rationally responding to the cost drivers. No wider inducement is involved. The approach may seem deceptively simple in its focus on a fairly straightforward equation, but proponents are convinced of its accuracy and eager—as well—to argue against the older explanations for British primacy. Finally, the emphasis on two factors in combination actually refers to a rather complex history, involving the evolution of wood use, the particular population structure, and earlier, if conventional, forms of economic growth and labor demand.

Beyond Britain

Many of the scholars focused on explaining British industrialization have scant interest in patterns of industrialization elsewhere. They may note some similarities with the British case that reinforce the factors they favor: for example, the importance of coal availability in Belgium and Germany, which would later follow the British lead. But the preoccupation with British distinctiveness reduces interest in wider Western patterns, much less later developments in other parts of the world. Deciding on the geographical and chronological target for inquiry, as we noted in Chapter 2, plays a huge role in determining what kinds of causation gains favor.

Explanations of British industrialization, finally, usually assume that producing the first Industrial Revolution, without an established model to follow, was a big deal, requiring powerful, distinctive causes. The alternative—that because British industrialization often featured fairly small firms and a gradual overall course it does not need an elaborate explanation—is not part of this picture.

The current state of the renewed discussion over British causation offers some truly striking features. Differences among historians are stark, and not always terribly polite. Advocates for the labor-and-energy argument simply see no value in the new State policy approach, and vice versa. There is some agreement on the importance of commercial growth prior to the eighteenth century: this plays a key role in both the wages and the government policy argument. And of course the new arguments emanate from British scholars, perhaps sharing a desire to restore attention to their nation in an age in which global industrialization is seizing center stage. But beyond that, the most recent claims have little in common. The question, why Britain first, remains vital in causation analysis, but definitive answers remain contested.

For further discussion

(1) Thus far, what seem to be the most compelling reasons that Britain was able to take the lead in industrialization? What additional factors might in principle be worth considering?

(2) Assess several key reasons that historical explanations often change over time.

(3) Should the energy/labor costs explanation for British industrialization be combined with other factors, or can it stand alone?

(4) Analyze the most important challenges to the institutional/ political explanations for British industrialization. What are the main recent additions to the government policy arguments, and how do they compare with earlier institutional analysis? How and why have discussions about the British government changed over time?

(5) In your view, what is the best current explanation for why Britain industrialized first?

(6) Why did the first Industrial Revolution begin in the eighteenth century, and not sooner, not later?

(7) How important is the question of Britain's industrial lead, compare to larger issues of explaining why industrial revolutions emerge anywhere?

Further reading

For the institutional approach see Douglass North, *Institutions, Institutional Change and Economic Performance* (New York: Cambridge

University Press, 1990) and *The Rise of the Western World: A New Economic History* (Cambridge: Cambridge University Press, 1973); quotations are taken from this second book. The most recent policy analyses can be traced mainly in articles: Patrick O'Brien, "The Nature and Historical Evolution of an Exceptional Fiscal State and Its Possible Significance for the Precocious Commercialization and Industrialization of the British Economy from Cromwell to Nelson," *Economic History Review*, 64 (2011): 408–46 and "The Political Economy of British Taxation, 1660–1815," *Economic History Review*, 41 (1988): 1–32. See also William Ashworth, *Customs and Excise: Trade, Production and Consumption in England, 1640–1845* (New York: Oxford University Press, 2003); "Practical Objectivity: the excise, state, and production in eighteenth century England," *Social Epistemology*, 18 (2004): 181–97; and "Quality and Roots of Manufacturing 'Expertise' in Eighteenth-Century Britain," *Osiris*, 25 (2010): 231–54.

On labor and coal see Emma Griffin, *A Short History of the Industrial Revolution* (Palgrave Macmillan, 2010) and (with a substantial and dismissive assessment of other factors) Robert C. Allen, *The British Industrial Revolution in Global Perspective* (Cambridge: Cambridge University Press, 2009). See also E. A. Wrigley, *Continuity, Chance and Change: The Character of the Industrial Revolution in England* (Cambridge: Cambridge University Press, 2009).

5

Debating the role of people and their motivations

A further set of causation discussions has emerged, during the past several decades, over the role of human factors in prompting industrialization. These discussions can certainly apply to the "why Britain?" question, but they are even more relevant to probing differences and similarities among industrial revolutions in the West more generally. This chapter explores arguments about the contexts and motivations for the people that actually shaped the industrialization process, both businessmen and workers.

We have seen that some accounts of industrialization assume that the actual participants responded fairly automatically to impersonal stimuli: enclosure movements (for workers) or increasing costs for charcoal or the specifics of tax policies (for manufacturers). There is no particular need to look further. Motivations gain little role as the human elements in the Industrial Revolution simply move as the impersonal forces require.

In contrast, explanations that include human options reflect a belief that automatic responses miss much of the point. Businessmen who innovated, to take the most obvious case, were not initially typical; their ability, even eagerness, to sponsor change must be distinguished from the reactions of others around them. Assessment of personal motives and characteristics become essential. This kind of analysis has prompted novel types of research. In one instance it also tied causation debates to an intriguing older argument about the consequences of Protestantism. Focus remains on Britain and the West, but now in the early nineteenth as well as late eighteenth centuries, and with the growing interest in national contrasts and comparisons as well. A specific comparison between Britain and France had generated particularly sharp debate over the role of human factors versus less personal inducements and constraints.

For from the 1960s onward, a number of historians began asking some new questions about key components of the causation list. They explored several additional elements in the conventional picture, correcting some earlier empirical errors, and they also probed some potential additional factors. The result was a crucial set of debates assessing the motivations of the people who actually set early industrialization in motion, and these debates continue to the present day. The first accounts of causation had not exactly left people out—after all, new economic theorists like Smith or Malthus were human beings—but they had not highlighted the role of the individuals and groups most directly involved in the process. This chapter focuses on the questions: do human motivations matter in this great transformation, and how can we get at them?

Most attention has gone to the entrepreneurial side, to explaining why some people and groups were particularly available to take risks and innovate. The role of inventors also prompted analysis, toward figuring out why some people began to introduce fairly dramatic technological changes. But it was also possible to take a second look at the early industrial labor force, to ask why some workers were available to assume new, often demanding and certainly challenging jobs, particularly when it became clear that some initial explanations of labor force involvement were off the mark.

Together, ongoing arguments about worker and businessman motivations create opportunities for serious attention to be given to the human sides of industrialization—or to the possibility that industrialization happened with no particular personal input at all, and was just a fairly automatic response to entirely impersonal factors. The analysis has been directly applied to the issue of differential responses within the West, with a spirited discussion around explaining a French "lag" in the process, compared to many of its neighbors.

Reconsidering the labor force: a limited debate

New discussions did not lead to claims that workers' motivations rose to the top of the list of industrial explanations, but they did raise important issues. There were several reasons for a new view. First, and quite specifically, additional research successfully challenged earlier assumptions about the role of the enclosure movement in the British process; and this in turn required additional analysis of where the new workers came from, and why they were willing to enter the factory system. Second, and much more sweepingly, the rise of social history, with its deep interest in understanding the lower classes as important agents in history, inevitably prompted deeper questions about what drew workers into the new factories. Earlier assumptions about almost automatic supply had to be rethought. It also became possible to wonder if workers played somewhat different roles in some of the different instances of industrialization, with France and the United States—to take the most obvious cases—showing patterns at some variance from those in Britain or Germany. Finally, questions emerged about particular segments of the industrial labor force—about women for example—or more skilled adult workers. And as we have learned more about the tremendous strain of early factory work, outlined in Chapter 2, the challenge to explain why and how workers accepted their assignments has intensified.

For any debate about the labor force assumes relatively bleak working conditions in the early factories. Without question, employers worked actively to keep labor costs down. Machines raised productivity, but the gains might be wiped away if other costs rose too rapidly. Furthermore, at least in employer eyes, machines simplified work for many employees, reducing (though not always eliminating) strength requirements and skill levels. Further, the machines cost substantial amounts of money, for manufacturers who did not usually come from highly affluent backgrounds; there was pressure to make sure the investments paid off quickly. This meant, typically, not only relatively low pay but also long hours at work (most early factories assumed 12–14-hour work days). It also meant extensive use of children—because they were cheap—though it's important to note that children had always worked in agricultural societies, so the innovation did not at first seem excessive. Other work conditions—more intensive supervision of labor by sometimes-harsh foremen, a machine-driven pace on the job—were often unfavorable as well. Overall, it is hard to see that many workers would be positively attracted into industrial jobs, though this should not be assumed without further analysis.

New questions about the sources of early factory labor arose in part because of more detailed empirical work on the British enclosure movement. There was no doubt that considerable British land was enclosed into large estates during the eighteenth century (after a previous round 200 years before), and the result surely encouraged agricultural innovation. But enclosure did not, the new research demonstrated, reduce the need for agricultural workers, whose numbers did not decline. Only much later would new agricultural machinery achieve that result. These findings also reduced the force of this angle of the conventional discussion of Britain's industrial lead; British labor supply conditions were less distinctive than had been imagined.

This turned attention to several related factors. Basic population growth was more important than land redistribution in explaining the availability of labor. British growth levels after 1730 were quite high for several reasons, but including the widespread adoption of the potato as an unusually efficient source of food. Enclosure, while it did not reduce agricultural numbers, did limit the ability of farming to absorb *more* people. But British labor supply (supplemented by Irish immigration) was not particularly unusual at this time—Germany, for example, featured similar growth rates—and there were parts of this region as well where large estates predominated. New population pressures pushed workers off the land in much of Western Europe, creating part of the context for industrialization, with Britain in this regard simply the first of many instances. The trends require caution in one respect: recent explanations for Britain's industrial lead emphasize that population growth did not prevent relatively high wages, which in turn helped motivate technological change; but it does help explain how a factory labor force became available.

The "push" factor of population growth does not close the discussion, however. It explains the mechanism, as people were pressed to take factory jobs because access to the land became more problematic, but several questions persist. First, it is obvious that population growth did not cause industrialization on its own. Without the several other factors generating technological change, growth might merely have increased poverty, as it did in many other parts of the world (including Ireland for many decades) at various points in the past two centuries. Labor supply becomes a vital component in a complicated list of causes, but probably not the decisive element.

Second, population structures were not identical in all early industrial settings, which allows further testing of this factor. Geographic variables may be considerable. We will see that France's relatively slow population growth was linked to a distinctively gradual pace of industrialization. The United States represents an even more clearly special case, with a much more favorable population-to-land ratio than that of Western Europe. This encouraged somewhat higher wages, to draw workers in, and also even greater employer interest in labor-saving technologies. With time, of course, surging immigration levels (by the 1840s from Ireland, Canada, and Germany particularly) and growing agricultural crowding generated a labor supply situation more similar to that of Britain. For a time, however, the challenge of attracting and keeping workers was an unusually active factor in American industrialization.

And third, probable variables within the labor force raise additional questions about employer reactions and about variations in worker motivation. Early industrial factories depended on extensive use of women, again because of lower wage costs. Rural population pressure plus displacement of traditional manufacturing by the factories themselves—for example in thread spinning—generated a considerable supply. Some women found factory work actively preferable to the main urban option of domestic service: they could meet more people and enjoy more latitude than when they were under the eye of a middle-class housewife. Skilled factory workers, though a minority, were another special category, needed for example in tending to the new machines. They received higher than average pay; they might have mobility opportunities, for instance into the ranks of foremen; and they might find the work unusually interesting. Here's another worker category that might have experienced special motivations and been "pulled" into new jobs rather than merely pushed by population pressure. On the other hand, some of the best paid early factory workers preferred to use their money to take time off or change jobs, more interested in recovering a traditional pace of work than in "getting ahead." Labor supply and the motivations involved could be complicated.

Inventors

Standard explanations of the Industrial Revolution often paid little attention to inventors, assuming they simply responded to opportunity. The most current explanations of "why Britain?", for example, though they may discuss inventions in detail, tend to assume that they simply responded directly to the need to counter relatively high labor costs and take advantage of cheap energy sources, or that they acted in response to opportunities created by government policy. There is little need to look at the process of invention itself. This may of course be correct, but it does downplay this aspect of the human factor.

At most, even when a larger canvas was available to deal with wider causal factors, historians referred to the importance of skilled craftsmen—"artisan tinkerers"—who manipulated traditional equipment to come up with new devices, like the flying shuttle in weaving. Britain might have provided unusual opportunities for the tinkerers because of relatively loose guild regulations to restrict innovation, but of course the tinkerers showed up in other societies as well.

The problem with the artisan-tinkerer approach is that it does not very clearly address the question of timing: why did the series of massive innovations begin in the eighteenth-early nineteenth centuries, and not before?

Three potentially related arguments have developed to address this question, beyond the assumption that inventors simply responded to opportunity, though each raises some problems of reliable evidence. First, some inventors may have been guided by exposure to products from other regions, and a desire to facilitate European manufacture in competition. From the sixteenth century onward, for example, European merchants traded extensively in printed cotton cloth, made in India; sales grew among European consumers directly.

Europe could not directly match the low wages of Indian artisans, but from the late seventeenth century onward various businessmen and inventors began to experiment with machine production that would expand output while keeping costs down and allow Europe to displace India as the source of this product. Inventors, in other words, may have been stimulated by the desire to catch up with, or outdo, other parts of the world, in a number of consumer product areas. This new approach potentially helps explain the timing of the initial surge in innovations.

Inventors may also have been encouraged by greater protections for intellectual property; as is often noted, why innovate if other people can immediately copy what you do? Britain established a new patent system in 1624, and many historians have speculated that this was one of the institutional changes that ultimately generated industrialization, by improving the incentive structure. Later economic theorists, like Adam Smith, insisted on the importance of patent protection, making another possible connection. The claim, however, faces clear empirical challenge. In the first place, patents may also block others from innovation by restructuring the availability of new technologies. Also, British patents were very expensive, and the government did not always enforce them well. Other countries, like the Netherlands, had patent systems, but actually lagged technologically under their aegis. Many actual British inventors did not take out patents, either because of the nuisance or because they really wanted the public to benefit as widely as possible. Some were more interested in winning public honors than in maximizing profit. A few patents did pay off—such as Watt's patent on the steam engine— but the overall linkage has been questioned.

Finally, inventors may have been encouraged by the new knowledge associated with the scientific revolution. This linkage, too, has been contested both recently and in the past. Traditionally, the fascination with the artisan-tinkerer model kept inventors largely apart from science, and at the same time there was a persistent belief that the scientific revolution was mainly abstract and theoretical, not open to clear practical applications; what inventions, after all, directly resulted from Newtonian physics? Recent critics have noted that the new science was widespread in Europe, in some ways more advanced in France than in England, which limits the applicability of this factor to the "Britain first" causation problem. But connections did exist. James Watt had a father who taught mathematics, and he himself made scientific instruments for the University of Glasgow. Might he not have been inspired by the scientific method, and by some specific discoveries on the expansion of gasses? Other inventions—for example in the bleaching of cloth—resulted directly from advances in chemistry.

Is there a plausible combination here that suggests that the heightened pace of invention was not merely a response to trends in energy and labor costs, but was more directly inspired by global trade examples, new scientific ideas and methods, and the existence of some opportunities for patent protection? Debate is clearly desirable.

Businessmen

Early industrialists often boasted of their dynamic spirit. A leading French businessman wrote of the "divine fire" that made him and his colleagues want to overcome all obstacles; others talked about their goal of "always expanding." Even factory owners who admitted how much they worried about innovation and failure may have possessed some special qualities that explain their persistence. Were innovative businessmen an accident, or (again) an automatic response to factors such as labor or energy supply or government policy (or, after Britain, to the opportunity for imitation of industrial example elsewhere)? Or can they and should they be explained?

A number of historians have tried to identify a special entrepreneurial quality that informed early manufacturers, and have sought to account for it. A few early factory owners rose from the lower classes, in the best rags to riches fashion. More, however, came from families that already had middle-class status (only a few were aristocrats). But obviously they innovated far more extensively than most middle-class people did, hence the idea of a special, driving spirit. Where did this come from, and why did it show up in the late eighteenth/early nineteenth centuries?

One explanation reached back to an older theory propounded by the German sociologist Max Weber. Weber had argued that

Protestantism unintentionally encouraged business drive, by making some people particularly eager to identify themselves as God's chosen and at the same time by encouraging sober saving rather than consumer indulgence. The Weber thesis thus associated Protestantism with the rise of Western capitalism more generally. Might this also apply to leading manufacturers? Britain, after all, was a Protestant country; could this be a factor in "why Britain"? Even in France, Protestant businessmen from Alsace took a disproportionate role in industrialization.

On the whole this approach, though interesting, has not survived well. Too many Protestants (for example, those in southern France) were not particularly dynamic, too much new industry would also develop in non-Protestant areas (like Catholic regions in Germany). But a related notion continues to draw interest: a disproportionate number of early businessmen may have been drawn from minorities, who were blocked from full social acceptance, including standard political careers, and so turned to new types of industry to make their mark. Studies in this vein of collective biography highlight the role of Quaker businessmen in Britain, Alsatian Protestants in France, even Old Believers (a dissident Eastern Orthodox sect) in later Russian industrialization.

Are there other ways that a special business spirit might be explained, or was this not an essential ingredient in the recipe for industrialization?

The case of France

Discussion of the human element is not just an abstraction: it has been applied directly to comparative issues in causation.

France did not industrialize as fast or as thoroughly as Britain (or Germany or Belgium) did. Growth rates were real—an old debate about whether France had an industrial revolution has largely passed—but they lagged. Where French industrial output rose tenfold between 1781 and 1913, British levels rose by a factor of 25; and German growth was as rapid simply between 1845 and 1913 as France achieved in 130 years. The question of course is why; causation applied to industrial diversity.

Argument one highlights the human element (inventors largely aside; France had some key inventions and was not really laggard here). Both workers and, more important, the middle class and business sector may (according to this argument) have had some special hesitations about participating in dramatic industrial change.

On the labor side, French population growth was considerably slower than Britain's or Germany's at 40 percent—in the nineteenth century—compared to 250 percent or more in the other two cases. France also featured a high degree of peasant landholding, rather than large agricultural estates. Lots of workers could and did prefer to stay in more traditional pursuits, and particularly on the land, so assembling factory workers posed some special difficulties. Many peasants, for example, may even have preferred a slightly lower living standard rather than packing up for the city, and widespread peasant proprietorship could permit this approach more readily than was true in Britain. French artisans, attached to well-developed craft methods and even a certain amount of artistry, may similarly have shied away from the factory scene, limiting the supply of skilled labor. Relatively slow population growth might explain greater worker conservatism; but it also might result from the same conservatism, the desire to limit change in order to preserve familiar arrangements.

But labor is not, usually, the key focus in the debate over the French industrial path. The human factor in France attaches far more to the business side of the equation. The level of entrepreneurial spirit, the willingness to take risks around new business forms and new technologies, is the real focal point. Here is where some historians, particularly the American David Landes, have hit hard. French businessmen, according to their analysis, simply lacked the drive to innovate, a few individual exceptions aside, according to this line of argument. They were more suspicious of technological innovation or rapid company expansion. And, in their eyes, they had more respectable alternatives, which is where the difference becomes potentially explainable. France was mainly Catholic, in case some aspect of the Weber thesis might apply. More important, the country also had a large but somewhat traditionalist middle class that found more conventional merchant activities more prestigious than manufacturing (which brought connotations of working with one's hands and other lower status features). Even more to the point, the French middle class may have particularly prized service in the State bureaucracy, toward which, among other things, graduates of the most famous institutions of higher education tended to gravitate. Here again, industrial pursuits would be comparatively less attractive, a less interesting target for social mobility for oneself or one's children. Businessmen, like skilled workers, may also have preferred the kind of production that emphasized more artistic qualities, where France had excelled in the seventeenth and eighteenth centuries—in furniture making, for example, or in silks or other expensive textiles that were in fact hard to mechanize. Prestige, for the French middle class or aspiring middle class, simply did not attach to economic innovation to the same extent as in Britain.

What might be called a human factors argument, then, contends that France suffered industrially—though not fatally; again there was change—because it included lower levels of the entrepreneurial ingredients crucial to industrialization. Britain, in contrast, had more of the ingredients—more population pressure, more entrepreneurial spirit, more positive zeal for change—hence the differential.

There is another explanation, however, that has nothing to do with human qualities. France also, by coincidence, has far less coal than its European rivals. It participates on the fringes of the great coal seam that supplies Belgium and Germany, in the north of the country; and there are pockets of coal elsewhere. But France had a harder time generating steam-based industrialization because the crucial resource was scarcer (and therefore more expensive). Only when other energy sources became available, notably electricity, could France fully take off. This was the great contrast with Britain, according to this line of argument.

The French case, thus, illustrates the dilemma of assessing the human components argument quite nicely: if the country had enjoyed abundant coal, would there be any need to assess labor proclivities or entrepreneurial spirit at all? Of course the arguments can be combined. Analysis can include the French challenge on the energy side but note that a somewhat distinctive business culture might have contributed to a slower rate of industrialization as well. It remains important to decide whether, on balance, culture and motivation gain primary emphasis, or whether other stubborn prerequisites, beginning with the components of steam-based mechanization, should be rated more highly.

Debates over the French "lag" and the comparative factors involved, involve weighing available evidence. They can also involve issues of time and place. It was probably no accident that the most vigorous attacks on French "entrepreneurial spirit" came from outside France, indeed from the United States where tradition often places particularly great stock on national entrepreneurial zeal. The analysis was careful: David Landes believed he had identified a crucial component, and not some artifact of national prejudice; but some extraneous cultural factors may have crept in. Needless to say French scholars, though not immune to exploring comparisons with Britain, tended to emphasize other explanations. And there was the question of timing as well. France ultimately would do somewhat better at industrializing—later in the nineteenth century—when hydroelectric power became available, and again after the Second World War. Does this modify the notion of some entrepreneurial deficiency, or is there still an issue?

People clearly participated in early industrialization. Equally clearly, they responded to some extent to impersonal factors like resource availability or government policy. The question, in explaining the Industrial Revolution, is what balance is involved. How much do we need to explore motivations as part of accounting for the onset of industrialization, and how much can we assume more automatic reactions to external stimuli? There's also, once again, the question of measurement. If we need to probe why some workers were willing to enter factories but not others, or the nature of entrepreneurial spirit, we are inevitably taken into a largely qualitative assessment, ideally looking for personal statements in evidence such as diaries or letters. But if the most important ingredients lie in the larger environment, as with coal supply, there is much greater opportunity for statistical data. Some historians, it's fair to say, are drawn to one style of analysis, some to another. What's the best, most accurate combination? The analytical challenge applies to industrializations in general, and to specific comparative cases—like Britain and France, or as we will later discuss, Japan and China.

For further discussion

(1) Do labor supply and worker motivation have much to do with explaining industrialization? Why and how did workers' goals vary? Do human factors have much to do with explaining "why Britain"?

(2) Discuss the case of French industrialization. Why have French patterns promoted a particular comparative causation debate? Is it possible to come up with a combined explanation that makes more sense than focusing on human elements or on natural resources alone?

(3) Discuss reasons for and against including scientific discovery in explaining industrialization.

(4) Define entrepreneurial spirit, and discuss the reasons it became more visible during early industrial revolutions.

(5) On balance, do explanations of industrial revolutions require assessment of human components and reasons for involvement in early factories and initial technological change? If human factors are downplayed, what causes substitute for them?

Further reading

David Landes, *The Unbound Prometheus: Technological Change and Industrial Development in Western Europe From 1750 to the Present*, 2/e (Cambridge: Cambridge University Press, 2003); Robert C. Allen, *British Industrial Revolution in Global Perspective* (Cambridge: Cambridge University Press, 2009); A. E. Musson and Eric Robinson, *Science and Technology in the Industrial Revolution* (Cambridge: Cambridge University Press, 1969); Joel Mokyr, "Intellectual Property Rights, the Industrial Revolution, and the Beginnings of Modern Economic Growth," *American Economic Review: Papers & Proceedings*, 99, no. 2 (2009): 349–55; Johann Peter Murmann, *Knowledge and Competitive Advantage: The Coevolution of Firms, Technology, and National Institutions* (Cambridge: Cambridge University Press, 2003); Christine MacLeod, *Inventing the Industrial Revolution: The English Patent System, 1660–1800* (Cambridge: Cambridge University Press, 2002); James Harrison, *Encouraging Innovation in the Eighteenth and Nineteenth Centuries: The Society of Arts and Patents, 1754–1904* (Toronto: High View Press, 2006).

6

Demand and education:
Two categories for debate

This chapter presents two factors that recurrently provoke discussion in explanation of industrialization: demand for goods, and education. Both relate to the assessment of the role of people and motivation, but they involve wider considerations as well. One— demand—may also tie into the question of the British lead in industrialization, though on the whole both education and demand apply more readily to discussions of the West more generally (and ultimately to industrial revolutions in other societies, like Japan, as well), rather than "why Britain?"

Schooling and consumer demand are not necessarily closely related. Both could combine in helping to explain industrial development. Debates over the two factors are usually separate, however, and so is the treatment that follows. We are dealing in both cases with components that seem very plausible, but in each case with interesting complexities attached.

Demand for goods

Lack of systematic attention to demand for manufactured products is arguably a striking feature of many causation discussions, both old and new. We have seen that the traditional explanations of the Industrial Revolution assumed that demand would exist for the increase in goods resulting from new kinds of manufacturing, but paid no attention to this as a new or contributing factor. The same applies, on the whole, to the debate over "why Britain?": explanations that focus on energy sources and labor again assume markets existed, but give this component no emphasis; government policy may link a bit more to consumer demand, in that higher import taxes might lead consumers to seek other, national outlets for production. Here too, however, the consumer sector is not seen as a real source of change. But, in terms of logical hypotheses, it is certainly arguable that the consumer sector should have been tested more carefully. And in fact, changes in consumerism—prior to the Industrial Revolution proper—have sustained one of the most innovative research areas in recent decades.

The question is a simple one: might the Industrial Revolution have been prompted, at least in part, by a realization that there were growing market opportunities for increased production? The conventional analysis that focused more on factors that prompted new technologies and work arrangements that fairly quickly increased outputs might be recast, to explore the possibility that potential reception for outputs itself might change. We know that later in the industrial process—for Western nations, clearly by the final decades of the nineteenth century—rising industrial production more clearly required adjustments on the demand side. Two vital results were department stores, as new mass distribution outlets, and the rise of professional advertising. But connections earlier in industrialization have not been as carefully explored, which long kept consumerism out of the causation debates.

In fact, demand could be shaky. Early industrial societies were not affluent. Markets for manufactured goods might falter, which is one reason industrial growth was sporadic rather than steady. Bad harvests, driving up the price of food, recurrently disrupted factory industry. To be sure, early industrialization tended to drive costs down—this was one of the goals of mechanization—and this helped open new markets or replaced more expensive handmade items. This pattern helps explain the tendency on the part of many historians to ignore demand as a causal factor in its own right. It is widely assumed that other factors prompted industrial revolution and that demand initially took care of itself.

Three new market sources are however worth considering. The most obvious resulted from population growth in eighteenth- and nineteenth-century Western Europe. Just as this helped explain the availability of labor so it undoubtedly helps explain how rising output could be sold. To the extent that businessmen understood population trends, they might well have found in them a positive incentive to sponsor industrial change.

Western merchants were surely actively aware of the second opportunity for market growth, in exports to many other parts of the world. Western Europe had after all been playing a heightened role in world trade since the sixteenth century. European shipping and commercial companies expanded rapidly once explorers discovered a route around Africa to Asia, and also crossed the Atlantic. At first trade consisted mainly of goods taken from the Americas, with silver at the top of the list, or of Asian products imported back to Europe or brought to other parts of Asia itself; European manufacturing had little to offer. Fairly quickly, however, Europeans began to export some processed goods, notably guns and decorative objects, to Africa in return for slaves; and sales of craft products like furniture to the wealthy in the Americas and Russia gained ground as well. It became increasingly clear that still further opportunities for manufacturing might exist, if European businessmen could find ways to undercut the costs of local production for items like clothing. This is precisely what early industrialization in textiles did, generating low-priced clothing that displaced tens of thousands of traditional handworkers in places like India and Latin America and in the process expanding export sales. Growing understanding of the potential of foreign markets might obviously have been a cause, as well as a result, of early industrialization, first in Britain but soon elsewhere in the West.

Finally—and most dramatically—the West itself began to undergo a real consumer revolution during the seventeenth and eighteenth centuries, in part because of earnings already brought back from global trade. While many people remained too poor to participate, a growing passion for consumer goods developed in most Western societies. Initially focused on food imports like sugar or coffee, by the eighteenth century consumer zeal expanded, embracing home furnishings including china, and stylish or colorful clothing; thefts of dresses and jackets increased, as one sign of the new passion. Acquiring goods became an increasingly important method of self-expression. Distribution systems responded, encouraging consumerism further in the process: small shops expanded, printed advertising emerged, shop windows became more enticing. There is no question that some manufacturers, at least, were actively aware of these changes. Josiah Wedgwood, a porcelain producer, kept careful tabs on consumer tastes, to take one example. He was exploiting a consumer area that had first developed in response to porcelain imports from China, but how he sought to make this an outlet for British products by constantly testing new designs and then expanding output for those that won consumer favor.

Historians' discovery of this birth of modern consumerism turns some aspects of industrial history on their head. Industrialization did lead to still further consumerism, as in the later nineteenth century, but it also may have been created in part by new, preindustrial consumerism that created obvious incentives to innovate, in order to expand production and increase sales. (It is possible that consumerism also helped motivate people to work harder—in order to acquire the means to consume—an explanation for new behavior by hard-driving factory owners and some workers alike.)

Attention to new levels of consumer interest links not only to the Industrial Revolution proper, but also to a preindustrial expansion of manufacturing in Western Europe, during the seventeenth and eighteenth centuries. Merchants began to recruit literally hundreds of thousands of hand workers to produce thread, cloth, metal tools and other consumer items, in what is known as the domestic or putting-out system. These rural workers used traditional, hand-operated tools and worked in their own homes, often part time while continuing to farm. This was not an industrial revolution, but rather what historians have called *proto-industrialization* or, as Jan de Vries puts it, an "industrious" revolution that would set the stage for the later, more dramatic technological change. Protoindustrialization accustomed many workers to the manufacturing process and to an increase in the intensity of work—with an accompanying decline in leisure—vital preconditions for the more modern and dramatic process of industrialization and to creating a factory labor force.

These changes were directly connected to increased consumerism as well, in two senses. First, demand for higher levels of production, for example in textiles, reflected a growing taste for manufactured goods. Second, workers themselves sought these new and demanding jobs because they wanted access to money wages in order to support greater consumption. Families were willing to work harder in order to meet changing expectations in demand. Additionally, experience in domestic industry, with attendant opportunities to earn money wages, fueled further consumer activity: domestic workers led their other rural colleagues in seeking access to colorful clothing and other items. These changes in turn—the experience with harder work in manufacturing, and the steadily growing demand that resulted from this work and the higher circulation of wages—set the stage for industrialization outright. Here was the transformation in supply that would at last be able to meet the new levels of consumer appetites.

Protoindustrialization and "industrious revolution" concepts link the Industrial Revolution directly to a prior set of Western changes in work and consumption alike, conceivably reducing the need to identify dramatic additional causes. We will see that similar concepts have been applied to other industrial revolutions, notably that of Japan. At the same time, the concepts raise issues about Britain's industrial lead, for the proto-industrial precedents were Western rather than purely British in scope. They also encounter complexities from more recent comparative work on Asian economic growth in the same period, as we will see in Chapter 7.

Putting consumer changes into the causation debates is obviously a complicated process, depending on new historical findings but also an expanded analytical range. As noted, it hovers uncertainly over the question of how much attention to pay to Britain first, as opposed to a wider geographic process. And it expands the attention we need to devote to the human motivation side of the explanation, which may be a good thing. But now we're trying to figure out why people started to want to buy more things, and how this affected manufacturers and workers, beyond the latter groups alone.

Education

Schooling and industrialization are unquestionably linked in some ways. Concern about conditions of child labor in early factories prompted reformers to seek legislation to not only limit hours, but to encourage if not require some education for the young people involved. Laws promoting schools—such as the Guizot Law in France of 1833—were associated with this kind of concern, and these would ultimately blossom into standard educational requirements as well as legal limits on child labor. This process took time—compulsory education in France did not arrive until the 1880s—and in some cases industrialization led to more schooling rather than the other way around. There is a clear cause and effect problem here.

Between the sixteenth and eighteenth centuries, literacy had clearly advanced in Western Europe—and it was also high among the non-slave population in the United States—though it was by no means universal. People were encouraged to read for religious reasons—this was an aspect of Protestantism, for example—but they also often read work-related manuals, about new techniques or methods to get ahead. In this sense educational advances contributed to the general framework in which industrialization occurred. This is not the same thing, however, as direct causation, and this is where the debate comes in.

For it is difficult to move from the general context of Western improvements in literacy and numeracy to a clear link between additional educational gains and the actual Industrial Revolution. There were no striking new developments in British education, for example, during the eighteenth century that might help explain the timing of the transformation. Indeed, British schooling was varied, probably a bit backward, compared to some other systems—the Prussian, for example—and no major historian has used educational advances as part of the "why Britain?" explanation.

Even for other countries the enthusiasm for education has arguably raced ahead of the actual facts. Some years ago Harvey Graff identified what he called the "literacy myth" in the United States: "the belief . . . that the acquisition of literacy is a necessary precursor to . . . economic development . . . and upward social mobility." His work has been picked up on by many other historians dealing with the United States and other countries (including Britain). The contention is that schooling remained quite limited and uneven when the Industrial Revolution began, even in the United States where attendance rates among the nonslave population were relatively high. Many early factory workers, including many women and in the United States many immigrants, could not read, and this did not clearly affect the quality of their work; remember that the typical factory operative was semi-skilled, and was largely trained on the job. While inventions were sometimes linked to exposure to science, as we have seen, others depended far more on direct craft experience. And though literacy probably supported skilled work for that essential minority of the factory population, even here it was not essential. Schooling may actually have contributed more to worker discipline—teaching the importance of punctuality and response to clock time, for example— than to explicit labor skills.

Obviously, these complications are debated, and no one denies that some educational gains formed part of the environment of early industrialization: it is simply hard to make precise or uniform connections. There is no question, also, that many reformers in early industrial societies *thought* the additional schooling was really important, no question also that, after a few decades of heavy child labor, schooling and literacy did begin to spread more widely. It is additionally possible that educational expansion was important for continued industrial development; that is a different issue from the debate over its role in launching the process of change in the first place. (Note: advancing literacy may also have been important to the further expansion of consumerism, for example in supporting the ability to read advertisements. It was certainly essential in preparing a larger white-collar labor force.)

There is one final complexity. Societies outside the West that sought to imitate successful industrialization often *believed* that advancing education was a vital first step. They were partly seeking to copy school systems they saw in the contemporary West, rather than carefully diagnosing the earlier Western situation when industrialization was new. Thus Japan, most notably, introduced universal education requirements in 1872 that produced a highly literate younger generation by the 1890s when the Industrial Revolution began to take off in that country.

Was education a more important cause in latecomer industrializations of this sort? There was more need to start from scratch to prepare a trained technical elite. In the West, technical skills including engineering had advanced more gradually, but in places like Japan, dealing with a less scientific Confucian culture, there may have been greater need to develop a more formal system in advance of further change. Even for the non-elite, as Japan worked to form its first factory labor force, some exposure to education may have been important to break through some other cultural barriers. Finally, latecomer industrializers, like Japan or Russia (where educational advance also occurred, though on a more gradual basis until after the Russian Revolution), had to introduce relatively advanced machinery if they were to be competitive with the West; they could not start small, as with Britain or even the United States. This might generate a need for more formal training. The role of education in industrial causation may in other words be different in particular cases, looming larger in more recent experiences.

Even here, however, some caution is needed: attention to educational reform, as it became a standard part of modernization efforts, did not always generate quick industrial response. If Japan is the clearest case of a probably positive relationship, Turkey, for many decades after initial educational expansion in the 1920s, stands as a more complex case. Schooling may expand, in other words, without quick industrial results. As with the role of consumerism, the historical debate continues.

For further discussion

(1) Define "modern" consumerism, and discuss its role in causing industrialization.
(2) Should consumer demand be considered more carefully in explaining why early industrialization developed, or are other factors adequate for the analysis?
(3) What is the proto-industrial concept, and how does it relate to explanations of the Industrial Revolution?
(4) Does the "industrious revolution" concept explain Britain's lead in industrialization?
(5) Why have so many people, policy makers and scholars alike, assumed that if an agricultural society installed a better education system, industrialization would follow? What are the arguments and the evidence?
(6) Why might education be more important, but new levels of consumerism less important, in explaining later industrial

revolutions such as the Japanese? What kind of demand did Japanese, or more recently Chinese, industrialization fulfill?

(7) What are the main issues in the debate over the role of education in causing industrialization? Using education and industrialization as an example, discuss the differences between context for change, and causes of change.

(8) Are consumer demand and education, as factors in industrialization, more useful in explaining the British industrial lead or in accounting for early Western industrialization more generally?

Further reading

On consumerism, John Brewer, Neil McKendrick, and J. H. Plumb, *The Birth of a Consumer Society: The Commercialization of Eighteenth Century England* (New York: HarperCollins Publishers, Ltd., 1984); and Peter N. Stearns, *Consumerism in World History* (New York: Routledge, 2001) on consumerism and world trade before industrialization. See also Beverly Lemire, *Cotton* (London: Bloomsbury, 2011). Refer to the important argument about the "industrious revolution" in Jan de Vries, *The Industrious Revolution: Consumer Behavior and the Household Economy, 1650 to the Present* (Cambridge: Cambridge University Press, 2008); for coverage of protoindustrialization, Peter Kriedte, Hans Medick, Jurgen Schlumbohm, and Beate Schempp, *Industrialization Before Industrialization (Studies in Modern Capitalism)* (Cambridge: Cambridge University Press, 1981). On debates over education: Harvey Graff, "The Literacy Myth at Thirty," *Journal of Social History*, 43, no. 3 (Spring 2010): 635–61; Stan Jones, "Ending the Myth of the 'Literacy Myth': A Response to Critiques of the International Adult Literacy Survey," *Literacy Across the Curriculum*, Centre for Literacy, Montreal, 12, no. 4 (1996): 10–17 (reprinted in *Working Papers on Literacy*, 1997); Peter Stearns, *Schools and Students in Industrial Society: Japan and the West, 1870–1940* (Bedford, 1997).

7

The global framework and new comparative debates

The most intriguing specific debates over the causes of the Industrial Revolution have taken shape over the past 15 years around a new (though contested) view of Europe's position in the world economy and the long under-appreciated economic vitality of China (and some other parts of Asia). The results have forced new thinking about why Europe industrialized first, ahead of Asia, because—at least according to many historians taking this new kind of global view—its advantages were far less systematic than was once believed.

This debate can be linked to several of the causation arguments we have already grappled with—for example—the discussions of British precedence. Other established ingredients include perspectives on factors such as coal supply, population growth or new levels of consumerism. And culture comes in for major reemphasis. But there are additional components as well in discussions that continue to seesaw. The consistent new theme, along with the reshuffling of familiar and less familiar ingredients, is the need to place the whole assessment of the Industrial Revolution in a far more global context.

And a final, smaller debate emerges as well, to be taken up at the end of this chapter: if, as seems clear, China maintained a far more dynamic economy in the eighteenth century than had been realized, equal or superior in many ways to the West, why did it not respond more creatively to the Western Industrial Revolution in the nineteenth century? This discussion involves negative causation, rather than explaining why something did happen.

Background: Europe, the world, and the world economy

Earlier economic and technology history provides vital perspective on the West and industrialization. Many historians, who clearly understood that the Industrial Revolution constituted dramatic change, nevertheless placed it in the context of previous European trade, capitalism and economic growth. Institutional explanations, for example, had highlighted the European small-government tradition, arguing that this had long provided latitude for cities and merchant groups to stimulate commerce and manufacturing. While some institutional arrangements were newer, like British patent law or the position of parliament after 1688, many historians pointed to earlier traditions of economic vitality that reflected special features of Western culture and politics. At an extreme, it might seem that ultimate Western industrialization simply built on earlier economic advantages Western societies had gained over other parts of the world over a long period of time. There was not much else to explain.

This approach has been widely and substantially revised, thanks above all to growing interest in world history. Western economies did gain ground in the thirteenth and fourteenth centuries, but they remained markedly inferior to leading Asian patterns. Measured by size of cities, urban living standards, or levels of manufacturing technology, the European economy, while changing, remained relatively backward. Any connection between earlier economic achievements and later industrialization are tenuous at best.

The situation did begin to shift during the fifteenth and sixteenth centuries, but relationships remain complicated. Europe unquestionably benefitted by embracing and improving upon technologies it learned from Asia, like explosive powder, the compass, and the printing press. However, the process of catching up more fully would take time. Important changes in trade position occurred thanks to European discovery and early colonization of the Americas, and particularly the opportunities to use silver mined in the Andes as a means of participating more widely in global commerce.

Indeed, key European countries began to develop a new system of inequality with some of their new trading partners, which was described thirty years ago by sociologist Immanuel Wallerstein in his work on world economy theory. Wallerstein saw France, Britain, and the Netherlands, in particular, developing a dominant position in world trade, partly through military force and colonization. These countries fostered commercial companies and shipping that monopolized exports from regions like Latin America and West Africa, earning disproportionate profits in the process; as we have seen, they also began to export some of their own manufactured goods, another source of profit. In turn, large stretches of the Americas lost ground in world exchange, exporting low-cost goods like timber and sugar (as well as silver), based on cheap labor, with weak governments and a rudimentary merchant class. West Africa became increasingly dependent as well, through the European-controlled slave trade. These regions would long lack the capacity to develop a more robust economy or to escape effective Western economic control. Even the Latin American wars of national liberation in the early nineteenth century did not do the trick. World economy theory provides a powerful explanation for the difficulty dependent regions would encounter in trying to develop industrial economies on the Western model: poverty, lack of a strong merchant tradition, weak governments and external influence would long hold them back.

World economy theory did not, however, capture a full picture of global trade relations during the sixteenth, seventeenth and eighteenth centuries. To be sure, Western profits from the new commercial role, and growing interest in generating manufacturing exports, would ultimately factor into industrialization, as we have seen. But world economic theory largely left Asia out, and the omission has proved critical in promoting more sophisticated, in many ways more challenging comparative research.

The "Great Divergence" debate

By the 1990s it was increasingly realized that China, and also India and at least some additional parts of Asia, had done far better economically during the sixteenth–eighteenth century period than most historians had understood. The glare of Western commercial success during the same period had distorted the picture, along with the fact that China did not reach out aggressively through merchant activity outside of Southeast Asia. But trade was brought to China in volume, by merchants seeking access to Chinese manufacturing exports. Indeed it was China, followed closely by India, that imported the largest amount of American silver in this period, brought by Western traders in payment for Asian goods. In earlier periods China had been an unquestioned world leader in technological innovations, witness explosive powder and the printing press. Now it turned out that its more recent economy had remained impressively dynamic as well.

This new picture results most directly from additional, careful research, which explicitly tested older assumptions. But it also took shape as contemporary China began its rapid trajectory of economic growth, becoming a leading global exporter. As is so often the case, current patterns of change help trigger revisions of history.

And the argument became more specific, particularly in the hands of historian Kenneth Pomeranz. Not only was China prospering, its businessmen were just as entrepreneurial as their European counterparts. Wages and living standards, Pomeranz argued, were also high, as were levels of manufacturing technology. There was an active consumer demand for goods. Rates of social mobility were just as dynamic as in the West. China, overall, was doing just as well as Britain by the late eighteenth century: the two nations were displaying some similar patterns of preindustrial economic expansion.

This in turn meant that European and British causation had to be revisited. The Industrial Revolution did not clearly result from older Western institutional patterns, for these had not pushed the West decisively ahead. It did not reflect a more appropriate political system. China's was different, but no less constructive from an economic development standpoint. In fact, some other historians added, the Chinese government interfered with the economy less than Western governments did, and levied lower taxes. Nor was Western culture measurably superior, for the facts showed that Chinese values supported business growth equally well. Chinese merchants cherished profits, they worked hard, and they planned rationally. And of course it had long been noted that China had abundant resources— particularly with coal—so a big Western resource edge made little sense either. Comparative data and analytical logic seemed to wipe out a wide range of earlier evaluation.

Yet Pomeranz and his colleagues did not deny that the West industrialized, and that China long did not. But if so many conventional explanations did not work, what was left to account for this ultimate divergence? The separation occurred later than previous analysis allowed: until the early nineteenth century China continued to hold its own economically, which was part of the challenge to older arguments that had assumed earlier Western advantage. But the break did occur. What causes were left?

Several factors worked in combination, in this new view. While China had coal, it may not have been quite as accessible as in the British case, so some elements of the resources argument could be salvaged. A population difference counted. Both Chinese and British/Western populations were growing, but Chinese agriculture was already more highly developed, which meant there was less margin for further change; growth in the lower classes thus strained resources and heightened poverty more than in the West. But the big difference, Pomeranz concluded, was British and European access to the Americas. Here was an outlet for part of the excess population, reducing the impact on wages. Here was a source of abundant resources, in silver and some foodstuffs, which would help support industrialization. The availability of cheap cotton, for example, would prove crucial for one leading growth sector, and China simply did not have this kind of advantage. The ongoing slave trade also provided a source of profits for the West. Expansion of American agriculture and raw materials production additionally generated a growing market for Western manufactured goods. Finally, while both Chinese and Western consumers sought new goods, the Chinese market was more saturated than that of the West, so an internal demand differentiation may have opened up. Changes in Western consumerism created more new opportunities, in other words. None of these factors alone explains the new contrast between Britain and China, but operating together they did the trick.

Other historians, working on the same revised comparative picture, came up with somewhat different explanations, as debate widened. R. Bin Wong, for example, placed much greater emphasis on political differences, but with a major new twist. He emphasized the contrast, by the eighteenth century and indeed before, between China's unified empire and Europe's network of competing, often warring states. Chinese rulers and elites featured policies that maintained the existing social order. This does not contradict the picture of economic growth and considerable prosperity: but there was less spur to move beyond a successful agricultural and commercial economy to something far different, particularly in terms of new technologies. European states had more reasons to accept change, as rulers sought new tax revenues and resources for their endless rounds of belligerent competition. The European state system also stimulated a more aggressive pattern of trade, which might affect business methods and culture more generally.

The new comparative picture also stimulated outright pushback. David Landes, long a leading student of Western industrialization, simply returned to the assertion that Europe had institutions, a culture, and an entrepreneurial spirit that were far different from what China had to offer. The Western Industrial Revolution flowed from these systematic and longstanding advantages, which generated the basis for new technologies and for successful marketing of goods around the world. And the process began clearly in the 1700s, in contrast to the tendency of the Chinese comparativists to place a measurable divergence only in the early nineteenth century. Landes simply rejected the new comparative challenge.

Recent efforts to explain the British lead also sought to refute key elements of the new comparative approach (though they spent far less time arguing about institutions and culture than Landes did). Robert Allen's emphasis on British energy and wage costs took issue with Pomeranz empirically. Most specifically, Allen points to more recent research that showed that Chinese wages were much lower than those in Britain by the eighteenth century. This means that the Chinese had no similar motivation to seek dramatically new, labor saving technologies. And differences in the nature of their coal resources limited the opportunities for an energy advantage comparable to that of Britain. Patrick O'Brien's recent work on the importance of the British government role also takes the global perspective into account (though he compares also to other European cases); thus he argues that British tax policy created more support for industrial change than occurred in China. Whether the emphasis is on government role or changes in energy and labor costs, the new view of China can be partially accepted, but modified enough to highlight a clear cut set of distinctive British ingredients.

Indeed, Allen's approach itself has been amplified, again in relationship to the larger comparative debates. Prasannan Parthasarthi notes that India simply did not face the challenge that arose in Britain because of the declining timber supply; this particular comparison, then, supports Allen's belief that a singular energy situation contributed strongly to the British pattern. A Japanese contrast also contributes in that Japan did encounter deforestation, but as the State responded by supporting new plantings there was no need—as a result—to seek coal as an alternative. On the other hand, Parthasarthi provides further detail about Chinese coal: not only was it abundant, it was actually used for fuel. He sees the crucial difference with Britain in government policy, not resource costs. The British government, and its navy, actively supported coal production and coastal transport, in ways the Chinese state did not. This was the basis for the growing availability of coal and its falling costs, hence its unquestionable role in British industrialization.

In various ways, then, debate continues on the basis of a new appreciation for a more complicated comparative picture. Choices mix disagreements about specific research findings with a reevaluation of new and old explanations directed toward explaining comparative differences.

Reviewing the components

Amid ongoing comparative discussion, several historians have tried to draw a distinction between recognition of the impressive economic developments occurring in eighteenth-century China, and the fact that, in their view, there were no signs "whatsoever" that any major technological breakthrough was on the horizon at that point. They are not fully disagreeing with the Pomeranz group, but rather placing greater emphasis on the magnitude of the "great divergence" and the difference between traditional growth patterns and the new type of modern growth inherent in an industrial revolution.

And this reemphasis could require a further review of causation, another look not only at the recent findings about China but at

Western factors as well, now with the comparative challenge firmly in mind.

One factor, already suggested, acquires much greater potential force. Knowledge of Asia's enduring manufacturing superiority, even as Europe gained a new role in world trade, calls attention to the growing awareness among European businessmen that they needed to think about how to catch up. While global commerce was profitable, by the seventeenth and eighteenth centuries it became increasingly clear that Europe might be doing even better if it could replace some of its Asian manufacturing sources. The result would be more direct sales within Europe, and possibly some new export opportunities as well. But catching up was not easy, particularly given relatively low wage rates in at least some Asian centers. The resultant combination—of new awareness but also the need to innovate in order to react successfully—might well motivate greater attention to technological change. Could a trend that was initially prompted by Europe's continuing lag in key branches of manufacturing, actually turn into a cause of the far more dramatic innovation embodied in the Industrial Revolution? Some historians distinguish between catching up and the causes of the real revolution, but a more dynamic connection might be possible.

Indeed one important study argues directly that it was competition with India—in cotton manufacturing—that opened the way to the larger industrialization process in Britain. Prasannan Parthasarathi puts it this way: growing imports of Indian cottons stimulated reaction from British business. It was vital to figure out how to produce thread at competitive prices, and mechanization was the only way to do this. Parthasarathi takes direct issue with the idea that the combination of high wages and low energy costs explains Britain's industrial lead, even though he explores the energy issue, because, he argues, this approach does not explain why so much innovation initially focused on the manufacture of cotton thread. Britain was trying to catch up with Indian advantages in this sector, expressed through the growing need to compete with imports, and this provided one of the key spurs to change. Once British cotton production began to take off, the British state added a further component by passing a law banning Indian imports—but by that point the wider transformation was already underway.

Part of the debate—again—involves timing: were eighteenth-century changes really part of an industrial revolution, or was this merely a prelude? Sociologist Jack Goldstone notes the huge strides in eighteenth-century Britain, not only in mechanizing cotton spinning, but also in generating a new porcelain industry for the domestic market (competing with Chinese imports) and producing more iron goods. But he adds "These were all striking advances for Britain, but in many ways were actually a catching up with the advanced civilizations of Asia, which already produced high-quality cotton cloth, porcelain, and cast iron." For him, Britain would install a real industrial revolution, but only with further developments during the early nineteenth century, and the essential causation lies elsewhere; eighteenth-century catch-up is merely a backdrop. But is a more connective interpretation possible?

Certainly the new comparative findings call for assessment and choice among some of the factors commonly advanced to explain Europe's industrial lead. Most obviously, many current scholars dismiss the still-lingering idea that Western industrialization built on a pattern of technological change that goes back to the Middle Ages. After all, given the fact that Western technology still lagged behind Asian levels, the argument that the West was somehow distinctively inventive becomes hard to defend.

The comparative framework may also complicate the more recent and focused arguments about protoindustrialization. If China's economy was also growing during the same decades that domestic manufacturing expanded in Europe, and in response to similar types of internal consumer demand, what then is the ultimate connection to industrialization, since the West experienced it and China did not? The Industrial Revolution becomes much less a logical outgrowth of prior change, even of prior consumerism, despite the attractive argument built by a number of economic historians of dealing with Western society just prior to the big transformation.

Another claimant—a distinctive European ability to control population growth—also comes in for critical scrutiny. Europeans did marry later than their Asian counterparts, but Asians controlled growth by different mechanisms, including infanticide; their average completed family size was not large by European standards. But debate remains: if this argument is true—and we are certainly learning to reexamine common stereotypes about Asia—does this mean that the idea of Britain as a high wage area goes out the window? Possibly it was not a special European family type, but the lingering effects of the massive population loss to bubonic plague (the Black Death) in the fourteenth century that created a distinctive labor cost framework. New insights on Asia do not resolve all the issues of fact; indeed, some become more acute.

Reexamining the role of religion presents an easier target, for after all considerable demolition of earlier theories in this area had already occurred. Claims that Christianity or more specifically Protestant Christianity offered a special basis for technological change—the old argument that this religion differed from others in urging the superiority of human beings over nature, and with this a distinctive basis for manipulating the environment—hardly holds up given our new understanding of how Asian societies often generated important economic growth. Buddhism, Islam and Confucianism all were compatible with advances in commerce and manufacturing, and there was no specific religious development in eighteenth-century Europe that can plausibly link with the emerging industrial transformation. At most—and this is a rather general statement—an atmosphere of growing tolerance in some parts of Europe and the colonies of North America generated a framework conducive to a new and unusually decisive round of economic change.

The new lens provided by a greater understanding of Asian dynamism also supports a critical review of claims about the Western state. Jack Goldstone, for example, offers a highly skeptical take on the argument that military and diplomatic competition among the European states created a distinctive openness to economic growth. He notes that India and Southeast Asia also had competitive state systems, but with no industrial revolution resulting; even some of the great empires, like the Ottomans and the Persians (Safavids) vigorously rivaled each other, but again without transformational economic change. He adds that Europe itself offers an obvious complication: while a few nations did turn out to generate industrial revolutions, others, including several with governments very involved in the process of military competition, like Spain and Portugal, did not. And of course stable, less competitive empires were quite compatible with economic advance, as the case of China abundantly demonstrates.

Finally, on yet another political front, it turns out that the British taxation rate by the eighteenth century was almost twice as high, per capita, as that of China, commanding 18 percent of the total national product; so much for the claim that a distinctively small government motivated by laissez-faire economic theory was a vital precondition to industrialization. Here, however, we have seen that a more recent approach to the State and taxation, from Patrick O'Brien, emphasizing a much more positive role, allows a distinctive take on this whole topic, highlighting special British political factors of a very different sort.

Several possibilities remain, on the political side. There is no question that the British parliamentary turn was distinctive (though the other main parliamentary state, Holland, did not industrialize early). The British system of common law may have been unusually resistant to arbitrary interventions by the government; again, a clear legal system may be an important precondition for economic innovation. And while British taxes were high, they helped support the large British navy that, in turn, helped clear the way for an expanded role in international trade, and greater reliance on coal. Still, many argue that it is hard to find a basic explanation for industrial distinctiveness in the political realm.

But if reassessment, and particularly reassessment based on the new understanding of the longstanding historical relationship between European and Asian economies, challenges or limits so many explanations, what is left?

A cultural turn

For several scholars, including Goldstone, the most important single explanation for the British and Western industrial lead, in light of the new Asian comparisons, lies in the cultural realm—in the development of new values and beliefs, in the seventeenth and eighteenth centuries, that in turn directly supported technological innovation. Goldstone points, first, to the emergence of greater toleration in key parts of Western Europe, including Britain, arguing that this is a historical precondition for economic growth. He notes that the most dynamic period of Arab trade, for example, had also taken shape around considerable tolerance, and he sees a corresponding relationship between heightened insistence on orthodoxy and greater economic stagnation (citing for example the later Ottoman Empire). This part of the argument may require further testing: Dutch tolerance was as great as British, but while it was consistent with commercial dynamism in the seventeenth century the relationship did not extend to a later industrial sphere. And continued Chinese economic growth, in the eighteenth century, occurred as the regime became less tolerant. Comparative assessments again introduce further complexities.

More broadly: what kind of culture can explain the widespread innovations that were integral to early industrialization? Goldstone returns to the importance of major developments in Western science in spurring the Industrial Revolution. He admits that many manufacturers remained unaware of specific scientific findings, focusing on more practical matters. And many scientists catered to a leisured class, interested in discovery but not in application. Nevertheless he insists on the direct links between scientific advance and key inventions such as the crucial iterations of the steam engine (both Newcomen's initial device, and Watts' later improvements). More generally, he sees the experimental method that was an essential part of the scientific revolution, particularly in Britain, explicitly applied in the eighteenth century to the search for many other new technologies, for example in cotton spinning.

But more than science was involved. The ideas associated with the Enlightenment were part of a wider culture of innovation that embraced scientists, craftsmen and many businessmen alike. A new idea of progress was fundamental: in Goldstone's words, "what transformed production was a generalized belief in the possibility, even the inevitability of progress and the conviction that such progress was in reach of anyone who pursued a systematic program of careful observation and experiment." This culture emerged from scientists eager not just to discover, but to popularize their results, but also from craftsmen newly interested in reading about the latest technological advances (a growing popular library system was crucial here) and for businessmen newly convinced that innovation was a social good. A new, widely-shared belief system replaced the more "traditional patterns" of intellectual life. From the scientific revolution, a growing number of people in Western Europe gained the conviction that new knowledge was more important than old; and it was this Western departure from the cultural patterns common in other parts of the world that explains the subsequent industrial transformation.

But there is one final, important twist, in Goldstone's view. While the scientific attack on intellectual traditions was a Western phenomenon, it was only in Britain that an experimental, instrument-based approach to science gained ground. Much of the rest of Europe, and particularly France, saw the new science more in theoretical and mathematical terms, with little or no connection to practical invention. British scientific leaders, in contrast, including the prestigious Royal Society, praised concrete experimental methods, and helped popularize them among a wider public, including craftsmen. Goldstone sees the dispersion of practical experimental knowledge as the crucial British ingredient. Comparisons within Europe, in other words, round out the picture of cultural distinctiveness directed at the larger challenge of explaining the Western divergence from Asia. Once Britain led the way, several other Western countries relatively quickly modified their own scientific approach to embrace more practical applications; this is where the wider implications of Western scientific culture kicked in.

The emphasis on fundamental cultural change as the precondition for a real industrial revolution touches base, of course, with several earlier analyses. Some relationship to educational advances may require new attention; how else were so many craftspeople able to pursue the new knowledge? Goldstone shies away from claims about a distinctive entrepreneurial spirit—after all, Chinese businesspeople continued to show a dynamism of their own in the eighteenth century, albeit in a more traditional overall economy—but some reminiscent implications resurface amid these new cultural claims. The role of the liberal economists does not survive—again, the key cultural changes started earlier—but they may be seen as reflecting the wider commitment to cultural innovation. The cultural package, in other words, now follows from the dramatic recasting of the comparative balance between Europe and Asia, but it may embrace some familiar components as well.

New stimulus, diverse response

New findings about Chinese and other Asian economies have unquestionably stimulated important reassessment of the basic workings of the Industrial Revolution. The picture of Europe's comparative economic position before industrialization has been redrawn. The challenge is unquestionable, a key example of how historical interpretations can be reopened by new discoveries and a wider global context. Equally obviously, the results have provoked renewed debate, not closure—and the debate touches base with a number of earlier discussions albeit in a new framework.

Obviously, the current comparative picture has disadvantaged some older interpretations, as certain factors no longer hold up. But the diversity of responses remains impressive, along with an interesting tendency to seek one or two basic explanations rather than—as in some previous renderings—a longer list.

There are disputes over the Asian findings themselves, both in general and around specific issues such as wage levels or population patterns. There are clear tensions between explanations that feature Western-Chinese differences, as opposed to those that single out Britain within the West. Most important are the ongoing debates over emphasis: does the key lie in European control over the Americas, or in the competitive state system, or in a peculiarly British energy cost/labor cost relationship, or in cultural change or some other factor entirely? Quite clearly, the jury is still out, even as ongoing debate stimulates further analysis.

Why not China?

The ongoing comparative debate, finally, raises obvious questions about what happened to China in the nineteenth century. If the new data are even approximately correct, China was at least near Western economic levels as late as 1800. But that certainly was not the case in 1900, when the West was moving toward advanced industrialization and China effectively had yet to begin. If it is legitimate to ask why it was not China, rather than Britain, that led in industrialization—given the many similarities in their eighteenth-century economic levels—it is even more urgent to figure out why China was not one of the first societies outside the West to join the industrial parade. It had industrial experience; its manufacturing had long been highly competitive in world markets; it also—a point increasingly emphasized—had capital, on the strength of past business success; and at many points in its history it had introduced and assimilated technological change.

Yet it clearly began to lag behind a number of other societies, even aside from the industrial West. Japan, Russia, and then later other parts of the Pacific Rim forged well ahead of China, gaining economic advantages preserved until the past 20 years. China was simply slow to move. At one point, in the 1870s, the government actually tore up some railway tracks an entrepreneur had built, an extreme gesture of hostility toward modern technology. Only in the 1890s did this attitude even begin to relent.

Some bad luck, and unfortunate external interference, explains part of this unexpected puzzle. Chinese government became notably less effective in the nineteenth century, a temporary lapse of a sort that had occurred previously in this great tradition. This reduced vitality in many sectors. It also promoted internal rebellion, and there was a huge and bloody rising in the middle of the century that was put down only with difficulty and that surely delayed any kind of response to Western example. External interference was a major problem. Britain led a war, beginning in 1839, aimed at forcing China to open its markets, not only to industrial imports but also to opium, which was being grown in India. This launched a new and serious problem for the Chinese themselves, as drug use began to spread. It also led to other foreign demands. Britain and many other countries forced China to grant long-term leases of many coastal territories, such as Hong Kong. These semi-colonies disrupted the Chinese economy and political structure still further. (A war with Japan, in the 1890s, was an additional blow.) Western holdings and other interference also encouraged resistance among the Chinese elite to any voluntary imitation of Western ways. Compared to several other societies, not only Japan but also the Ottoman Empire, China proved to be extremely slow and reluctant in embracing any kind of reform. And that of course included any systematic effort to generate an industrial revolution.

Does this set of factors adequately explain why, as one historian put it, China "struggled" to modernize? It would ultimately take a major revolution and then a communist seizure of power (after the horrendous experience of the Second World War), and then a renewed commitment to reform to begin to generate full-scale industrialization, by the 1980s. Or does China's struggle suggest some deeper factors that should cause a further review of the Chinese-Western comparison earlier on? Was China too averse to serious international involvements (except for trade brought to its shores) to be a plausible early industrializer? Were there some wider cultural factors after all, some further weaknesses in the Chinese cultural traditions? Was a state that had rejected international commercial expeditions in the fifteenth century capable of tolerating full bore technological change, as opposed to a steady but more gradual growth of a more traditional economy? Here, on the negative, or "why not?" side, is another important series of causation questions.

Certainly, the developments in nineteenth-century China raise a different kind of comparative debate: why Japan, and not China? For by the later nineteenth century it was Japan—which shared a number of characteristics with China, but enjoyed far fewer natural resources and a much more systematic pattern of previous isolation—that next moved toward industrialization. We turn to causation questions in some key latecomer industrial revolutions in the following chapter.

For further discussion

(1) Review the earlier explanations for industrialization that had to be reevaluated in light of the new findings about China. Which now should be dropped, and which ones are still worth considering? How do new understandings about premodern Asian dynamism affect explanations based on: resources and population; consumerism; the role of the State; the role of culture?

(2) How and why have views about European and Asian economic levels before the nineteenth century changed, and what impact has this had on earlier causation approaches?

(3) "A historian, of course, lives through time himself, and the world changes in the course of a lifetime . . . quite drastically . . . so that your awareness . . . will alter if you keep reading and keep listening and keep talking to people. . . So you're never the same twice. No day you're quite the same person. Your sensibilities and what you can see in the world will alter . . . and thus history will always have to be rewritten." (William McNeill, interview with Oregon Public Broadcasting, *Bridging World History*, February 2004. The interview was part of a series on reevaluations of the Western role in world economic history.) How have changes in the world over the past three decades affected the kinds of questions historians ask about the Industrial Revolution?

(4) Do the changes in the understanding of Asia's economic position on the eve of industrialization force radical shifts in explanations of the early Industrial Revolution? Why, or why not?

(5) Does the idea of Europe's trying to catch up with Asian manufacturing help explain the origins of the Industrial Revolution?

(6) What are the strengths and weaknesses of the cultural approach toward explaining industrialization? What earlier explanations might be linked to the cultural dimension?

(7) Review the causes Pomeranz adduces for explaining the "great divergence". Are they adequate to explain the magnitude of change?

(8) Do the new discussions about causation reflect a wider process of uncertainty over Western values, in a post-imperialist age?

Further reading

Relevant work on the global context includes Immanuel Wallerstein, *The Modern World-System II: Mercantilism and the Consolidation of the European World Economy, 1600–1750* (Berkeley and Los Angeles, CA: University of California Press, 2011); see also his briefer treatment in *World Systems Analysis: An Introduction*, 3/e (Durham, NC: Duke University Press, 2004); Prasannan Parthasarathi, *Why Europe Grew Rich and Asia Did Not: Global Economic Divergence, 1600–1850* (New York: Cambridge University Press, 2011). On reconsidering comparative issues with Asia, see Andre Gunder Frank, *Re-ORIENT: Global Economy in the Asian Age* (Berkeley and Los Angeles, CA: University of California Press, 1998); and especially Kenneth Pomeranz, *The Great Divergence: China, Europe and the Making of the Modern World Economy*

(Princeton, NJ: Princeton University Press, 2000). For David Landes' response to claims about China, see *The Wealth and Poverty of Nations: Why Some are So Rich and Some So Poor* (New York: W.W. Norton and Company, Inc., 1999). See also Piet de Vries, *Escaping Poverty: The Origins of Modern Economic Growth* (Göttingen: V&R Unipress, 2013); and Bin Wong, *China Transformed: Historical Change and the Limits of European Experience* (Ithaca, NY: Cornell University Press, 1997).

An important analysis of the West in comparative context is Jack Goldstone, *Why Europe? The Rise of the West in World History 1500–1850* (New York: McGraw-Hill Humanities/Social Sciences/Languages, 2008). A convenient summary of some aspects of the debate is Patrick Manning, ed., "Asia and Europe in the World Economy: Introduction," *American Historical Review*, 107 (2002). On China's later economic problems, as it faced a newly-industrial West, see Michael Gasster, *China's Struggle to Modernize*, 2/e (New York: Alfred A. Knopf, 1982).

8

Industrializing late:
Adjusting the causes

Latecomer industrializations—with Japan's heading the list—generate their own demand for explanation. Several themes predominate. First, of course, is the question of what factors carry over from the classic cases of industrialization. To what extent did Japan, for example, reflect the same kinds of causes that had operated in Britain, simply with a century's lag in time? But second is the issue of compensation: inevitably, latecomer industrializers could not and did not exactly replicate the British ingredient list. What components were available to make up for any gaps? Both of these basic questions are of course complicated by the ongoing debate about Britain itself, as well as the other early Western industrializers. If we cannot fully agree on what caused the first Industrial Revolutions, how can we adequately compare the latecomer formula? But it is possible that exploring later examples will actually help sort out the existing debates. The tension can cut both ways.

Always—and this is the third theme—discussions of the reasons for latecomer industrial revolutions must include the question of why these regions and not others? What was Japan's edge over other parts of Asia, to take the most obvious example? Industrialization did begin a significant geographical expansion by the end of the nineteenth century, but from a global standpoint it remained uncommon for many decades still. What are the key differences between the new arrivals and the nonstarters?

Overall, latecomer cases significantly expand both the opportunity and the need to debate causation. Having additional examples allows further tests of some of the themes already generated through the examination of the earlier industrializers: there is simply more information, more opportunity to select or reject options. But the need is vivid as well: new industrializations in the late nineteenth and mid-twentieth centuries did not happen automatically. They have to be explained, through some combination of familiar factors and compensatory components.

Picking the latecomers

A number of societies began a clear industrialization process by the later nineteenth century, in several key regions. Portions of southern Europe, for example, accelerated the pace of economic change. Russia began its Industrial Revolution, though it would intensify after the 1917 Revolution, under communist leadership. Industrial centers also sprang up in some other parts of Europe. As before, each pattern had its own distinctive features, based among other things on available natural resources. Many were spurred by a prior development of a rail system, which facilitated the movement of goods and materials and created a direct demand for heavy industrial products.

Russia's early Industrial Revolution was an obviously important development; the sheer size of the nation gave it a prominent place in global manufacturing levels by the early twentieth century. Not only an expanding rail system, ultimately capped by the great trans-Siberian line, but also a reform current that in 1861 ended formal serfdom and facilitated the movement of labor, while setting the stage for further change. Government encouragement was vital. Favorable resources included not only substantial holdings in coal, oil, and iron, but also direct access to raw materials like cotton, produced in the empire's central Asian regions. Like the other European latecomers, Russia participated actively in the competitive European states system, which generated clear military motives to promote industrial change, particularly in heavy industry; indeed, it was defeat in the Crimean War (1853–6) that helped impel the reform movement. The nation also had established patterns of contact with Western

Europe. This had already opened elite culture, and elite education, to the findings of the scientific revolution, creating at least some of the cultural components relevant to industrialization. Established exchanges also promoted an active role for Western businessmen and some skilled workers in Russia's initial industrial development. Capital and management arrived particularly from Germany, Belgium, and France, but even key United States firms set up branch operations. The Singer Sewing Machine company had a major Russian outlet, while the father of the American painter Whistler provided engineering services in designing early rail systems. By the early twentieth century a full half of all Russian industrial firms were foreign-owned.

Russian and other latecomer European industrializations obviously contribute additional examples of effective causation, almost always involving significant imitation of established industrial patterns and considerable government involvement, deriving in part from a desire to improve competitive position in the European state system.

Japanese industrialization, also beginning to take shape by the 1890s, involved some distinctive complexities among this latecomer group. In contrast to the European cases, Japan had no record of extensive contacts with the West; exchanges during the sixteenth century had been cut off in favor of substantial isolation. To be sure, there has been some debate over the extent of isolation, with the possibility that more export activity had persisted than scholars have commonly realized. And Japanese translators did maintain contact with Dutch merchants (the only group allowed even limited access). Through this medium, some Japanese leaders gained a certain awareness of intellectual developments in the West; indeed, during the eighteenth century rules changed to allow translation of European work in science and medicine. But this was limited exposure at best, compared to the regular exchanges among all parts of Europe including Russia. In no sense did industrialization spring naturally from a long pattern of interaction. This in turn suggests that the Japanese Industrial Revolution requires particularly careful causation analysis, including the debates that inevitably attach to this effort.

Japanese industrialization was followed, though several decades later, by industrial revolutions in several other East Asian societies, headed by South Korea and Taiwan. Explanations are somewhat more obvious than in the Japanese case, in part because by this point

Japan itself provided both a model and a market. But some factors overlap with the assessment of Japan, extending "Why Japan" to "Why the Pacific Rim."

First debates: industrialization itself

Japanese industrialization raises some definitional questions rather like those applied to Britain earlier, and with some of the same implications for causation. One issue was at what point preliminary technological changes in some key industries morphed into a more general transformation process. Japanese scholars have recently emphasized the important continuities in more traditional industries, even as some mechanized areas emerged. Whereas previously there had been substantial agreement that an industrial revolution took off around 1885, when initial rail lines were complete and the number of new textile firms expanded, now there is some sense that the real launch did not occur until after 1900. Even then, a great deal of domestic manufacturing persisted; indeed it was only after 1910 that modern factory production accounted for half of the total manufacturing output. Not only brewing and food processing, but also a good bit of hand weaving held on strongly. So is the Japanese transformation an abrupt process or a more gradual and complex evolution? A decision here, as we will see, can strongly color analysis of causation.

Obviously, this aspect of Japanese industrialization links directly to some of the key debates around the process in Europe, perhaps particularly in Britain and France. We have seen that the British Industrial Revolution did not sweep through the entire economy right away, while French transformations were even more selective. Figuring out how to balance the extent and range of Japanese, or later Korean, change with ongoing continuities fits into a standard analytical challenge; but the questions remain important.

On the other hand—and here there is a decided difference from the British case—Japanese and, even more, later Pacific Rim industrializations, once they got going, happened relatively fast: not overnight, but in the space of a few decades. Some scholars in the region talk about "compressed" modernization or industrialization, when comparing to previous Western patterns. Causation here has to account for speed.

The role of resources

One component, much discussed for British industrialization, seems strikingly absent in the Japanese case. Japan was not blessed with relevant resources in any abundance. There were some coal holdings, but even early industrial development made it clear that Japan would have to import energy from elsewhere, a situation that still applies today. This added to the costs and challenges of industrializing in the first place. To be sure, Japan's abundant coastline encouraged shipping, once the nation reopened to international trade. And a quickly-built rail network facilitated transportation among the islands. Not only energy but many other raw materials had to be brought in from other regions. One of the reasons Japan's Industrial Revolution featured a strong emphasis on exports was the obvious need to build up earnings in foreign currency to pay for essential imports.

This situation does not, of course, disprove the importance of resources in other cases, such as Britain's. Each industrial revolution features some shared causes, but also distinctive patterns. It does mean that explanations for Japanese industrialization need to account for the motivations, or other compensations, that would allow the nation to overcome this additional hurdle. In the circumstances, the achievement was all the more considerable.

Imitation and competition

Like all latecomer industrial revolutions, Japan's benefited from the opportunity to copy more advanced machinery and organizational forms. There was no need to experience the demanding evolution from simple machinery to more efficient versions that describes British or Belgian industrial history. It is important to remember that not all manufacturing sectors converted to the more efficient technology right away; Japan long mixed labor-intensive and relatively high-tech operations. Still, there was an opportunity to achieve some striking productivity gains in some sectors.

Against this advantage came the challenge of competing with far more advanced Western economies, a challenge all the greater in that Japan urgently needed to find export markets for some of its goods. It was not easy to break through in some of the areas where Britain had experienced such striking gains in its early period. Cotton manufacturing, for example, was highly competitive. This overall challenge was enhanced by considerable Western interference in Japanese affairs from the 1850s, when Western warships pressured Japan to open its markets to the outside world, until the early twentieth century. Japan was not free, for example, to set its own tariffs on imports until 1911. Obviously, the nation did find a way to industrialize despite these barriers, relying on a combination of new technologies and low labor costs, but it was not easy. Again, explanations of Japanese industrialization need to identify some powerful stimuli.

"Native" vs. imported: the role of protoindustrialization

Debate over Japan's Industrial Revolution has featured important evaluations of the role of preindustrial trends. This perspective offers some striking overlap with some of the analyses of the earlier Western case. How much do industrial revolutions flow from prior, if un-revolutionary, economic change?

Many historians have investigated important advances toward a more capitalistic, commercial economy in the two centuries before the 1850s, during the period when Japan was ruled by a regime called the Tokugawa Shogunate. One scholar claims that Tokugawa Japan, along with premodern China and Western Europe in the seventeenth and eighteenth centuries, are the only cases in history of "intensive" economic growth before industrialization. Manufacturing expanded. More farmers and fishermen began producing for commercial sales. Prosperity rose. Particularly important was the growth of rural industry, in a protoindustrial pattern quite similar to that developing in early modern Western Europe. All of this occurred despite Japan's considerable isolation, though there is also the debate over the possibility that the nation managed to export more than had previously been realized.

Several other findings bolster this argument about an important link between prior changes and the ultimate capacity to industrialize. Before the later nineteenth century (and in contrast to China) Japan had managed to control population growth. This meant that the expansion of domestic industry could generate some improvements in wages. More obviously still, protoindustrialization meant that there was a considerable pool of Japanese labor that was skilled and accustomed to market-based production. Finally, and this is a related point, the Japanese population was relatively well educated. Only a minority could read (and far more men had this ability than women), but the percentage of the literate population prior to the later nineteenth century was probably greater than in any region other than Western Europe and the Atlantic coast of North America.

This approach to Japanese economic development sees the ultimate Industrial Revolution as a real revolution—but one that flowed from preexisting trends—not primarily an importation. Japan, according to this view, had its own economic strengths, and it would be a mistake to apply a Western Industrial Revolution model too mechanically. Protoindustrialization created new divisions of labor and specializations, albeit in the context of domestic manufacturing, that were directly relevant to later industrial capacity.

Extending this argument, historians like Nakamura Naofumi not only see Japanese industrialization as a native product, not a Western import, but also downplay the importance of government initiatives as opposed to spontaneous local business capacity. Protoindustrialization created an interest in economic advancement not only at the level of the central government, but also in the provinces "where it manifested itself as a combination of nationalist sentiment and aspirations for local development. The most salient feature of provincial enterprise was the strong impetus of local initiative in the procurement of funding and human resources. Local bureaucrats and men of influence often took leading roles. The successful launching of enterprises in provincial areas was facilitated by two factors: the provinces had already grown socially competent to pursue industrialization, and the development of rural industry since the Tokugawa period had made them fairly affluent."

No one would deny that Japanese industrialization incorporated some outside influences, that helped shape key reforms—like the establishment of new educational requirements—and that provided guidance in mechanization. The ability to import advanced equipment, for example railroad locomotives, was crucial to the industrial launch. But Japan controlled foreign business far more carefully than Russia did, during the later nineteenth century, and it is obviously possible now to debate how much foreign example was needed.

On the other hand it is worth noting that Japan did also benefit from a tradition of successful imitation, copying foreign patterns but without losing local identity. This had occurred in interactions with China before the Tokugawa period, and some historians argue that this provided a crucial precedent for interactions with the West during early industrialization. They contrast this Japanese tradition with China's lack of comparable experience. The debate over "native" base versus the importance of foreign example continues.

Government role

As we have seen, almost all accounts of latecomer industrializations argue that governments play a greater role in spurring and guiding the process than was true in the pioneering cases. Governments must provide some of the elements that were more spontaneously available in Britain and other parts of the West. Thus their taxing power was essential in raising capital, in countries that had less elaborate banking facilities and private wealth. Japan had only half the level of per capita income of Germany, on the eve of industrialization, which made State access to resources arguably particularly important. State initiative, including directly establishing and operating some of the initial factory operations, helped substitute for a lack of comparable private enterprise. Governments might also have to introduce some more general reforms, to help clear the way for industrialization to begin; Russia's abolition of serfdom was a case in point.

The argument can be overdrawn. We have seen that even in Britain the State's involvement was critical in many ways. It was a government measure than banned Indian imports, helping to encourage the domestic cotton industry; government protection also promoted the expansion of coal production. Government backing ranged from new transportation projects, to improvements in banking, to police measures that inhibited labor protest. Even taxation seems to have played a role. The points about latecomer governments may well be true, but the contrast may be more subtle than is sometimes recognized. Comparing government roles—broad similarities as well as differences—is a crucial subset of the larger topic of comparative causation.

For Japanese industrialization, debates over the government's role range even more widely On the pro-government side: even before full industrialization the State had run a number of enterprises, and while it turned many of these over to private hands in the 1880s and 1890s it retained arsenals and railway workshops, which proved to be leading disseminators of advanced technology and management methods, in turn providing models for private business. In 1901 the Japanese state set up the nation's first and largest steel mill, the Yawata Iron and Steel Works. The government also sponsored many of the negotiations with foreign banks and businesses, another key element in Japanese industrialization. More broadly, State initiatives such as the 1872 education reform, with its required school attendance, contributed greatly to the development of a relevant labor force. The government also played an active role in encouraging private savings, a key source of investment funds, notably through setting up a postal savings system in the late 1890s. Even today, Japanese savings rates are quite high, but this may be a reflection of the government's intervention rather than an ingrained popular tradition.

On the cautionary side: obviously, the new emphasis on Japan's preindustrial vitality tends to downplay the importance of State intervention. Japan already had some wealth and capital, and it certainly had a strong business tradition. While some State enterprises helped guide wider industrialization, others were outright failures. Many State businesses prospered only when they were turned over to private hands. In textiles, the government did set up factories but for the most part they were poorly run. Breakthroughs, for example in cotton spinning, came from private firms, including the activities of key industrialists like Shiusawa Eiichi, a former peasant. According to this argument the State did provide a favorable environment for largely private activities, but that was about it. An entrepreneurial spirit was clearly present outside government ranks.

Similar arguments apply to the State's military role. Military concerns undoubtedly help explain why Japan moved so quickly to reform measures, including support for early industry. The possibility of Western military intervention, from the arrival of American warships in 1853 onward, directly triggered the wider process of change. Japan had not been part of the European competitive network, but its State traditions and emphasis on military qualities may well help explain why the country was quicker than some others in recognizing the need to respond vigorously to the industrial West.

More specifically, as Japan rapidly turned to the development of a modern military during the reform era, government purchases helped stimulate industrial growth. Naval yards were centers of technological change, which could affect other sectors. Many of the great industrial combines had close ties with the military. Imperial expansion, beginning with military victory over China in the 1890s, gave Japan a new empire, soon including control over Korea, which provided access to cheap raw materials and markets for Japanese goods. Victory over China also gave the government a huge indemnity that contributed directly to capital formation.

On the other hand, military endeavors cost money that might have been devoted to other purposes: it may be no accident that Japan's most dramatic economic growth occurred after defeat in the Second World War and substantial demilitarization. Military adventurism most clearly distorted the economy during the 1930s and the Second World War, but there is debate over the military role even in early industrialization.

Overall, recent analysis has raised an impressive number of questions about the importance of State initiatives, against the conventional backdrop of generalizations about latecomer patterns. Causation in Japan, correspondingly, may have been less distinctive, compared to Western precedent, than was long imagined. Not only prior economic development but also a supportive culture may count for more than unusual State initiatives: this is part of the ongoing debate. But if culture plays into the mix, this raises comparative issues of a different sort.

Culture

The role of culture in causing Japanese industrialization is both surprising and unsurprising. The importance of culture in many of the arguments about Western industrialization, including Jack Goldstone's recent analysis, makes it logical enough to seek a Japanese counterpart. But most of these arguments assumed Western distinctiveness: as we have seen, it was the contrast with the traditionalism of other cultures that was the main point. Part of the argument about the importance of government intervention, after all, assumes that Japan lacked a culture of change, so that the impetus had to come from other sources.

But a more complex culture argument has emerged. It is of course encouraged by the greater understanding of preindustrial economic dynamism: after all, if the Japanese economy was growing earlier, its cultural traditions must not have been entirely restrictive. But as we have seen with China-Western comparisons, compatibility with economic growth is not the same thing as compatibility with economic transformation. The culture argument needs some next steps.

The focus is on Confucianism. Japan was not culturally monolithic on the eve of industrialization. The country had its own religious tradition, in Shintoism, complemented by an important Buddhist element initially imported from China. Increasingly over the previous two centuries, however, Confucianism had predominated, sometimes in combination with religious belief, sometimes separately. The turn to Confucianism was intimately connected to the maturation of the Tokugawa regime, with its emphasis on effective central governance. While some cultural diversity persisted within Japan, the Tokugawa period cannot be seen as a full example of openness and toleration, and this aspect of the Western cultural argument has not been applied to Japan.

Confucianism itself, however, arguably played its own role in industrialization—not because it substantially resembled the cultural framework created by the Western scientific revolution, but because it offered a different set of supports.

Western scholarship had long dismissed Confucianism as a "traditional" value system which of course is true. The philosophy was first devised in China 2,500 years ago, and while it underwent various changes and emendations, and in the process was gradually exported to other East Asian societies including Japan, there can be no pretense that it offered revolutionary novelty. Indeed, one of the key issues in treating Confucianism as an industrial cause—in obvious contrast to the arguments about the scientific revolution in the West—is that on its own it involved no striking preindustrial innovations, which might cast doubt on its relevance to the timing of the economic transformation of Japan.

But, in part to emphasize the Japanese rather than purely imitative process of this latecomer industrialization, a plausible argument has emerged. First, as noted, Japan did become increasingly Confucian in the two centuries prior to its Industrial Revolution; and some have argued that Japanese Confucianism itself shifted somewhat, which might have some bearing on the readiness of the nation's elite to accept change. There was cultural change before Japanese industrialization; it was Confucian rather than scientific, but it still might have a real role in what came next.

More generally, Confucianism, even in a more traditional version, did offer a number of qualities that could build into the industrial transformation. It was secular, rather than otherworldly, valuing positive social conditions here and now. It offered real faith in human capabilities. It emphasized the importance of hard work and contributions to social wellbeing. It also stressed the importance of harmony and obedience, which could contribute to stable relationships even amid economic change. It argued against narrow self-interest and accepted the importance of government leadership. Finally, Confucianists had long valued education—not modern education, to be sure—but they held an esteem for schooling that could apply to modern offerings as well.

Obviously, this was a different set of cultural virtues from those touted by Western innovators. The point is, according to this cultural causation argument, that Confucian qualities, precisely because they were different, provided a distinctive but equally relevant basis for industrialization. Certainly, not only government leaders but also individual entrepreneurs, like Eichi, during the early industrialization process, made almost exactly this claim: devotion to the social good and the state, rather than maximum personal profit, were their proclaimed motivations for sponsoring dramatic economic change.

And there is one more piece to the puzzle that may provide the missing element of cultural adjustment within a Confucian context: Japanese reformers successfully introduced two key changes into the Confucian tradition, during the 1870s. Educational leaders like Fukuzawa Yukichi, fresh from visits to the West, urged that two aspects of Confucianism needed immediate correction: first, the lack of adequate concern for scientific research and application; and second, a tendency to devalue new knowledge in favor of older wisdom. The whole of Western culture was not embraced: as one East Asian historian, Tu Wei-Ming, has argued, "the dynamism of the modern West may have become the envy of the rest of the world, but its cultural specificity makes it in a substantial way non-exportable." Japan retained Confucian beliefs in the importance of government, social cohesion, respect and obedience, for a long time explicitly rejecting Western values in these areas. But the combination of genuine cultural innovation, in immediate connection with the timing of early industrialization, and the values that Confucianism would otherwise bring to the industrialization process provides a powerful—if different—cultural context for Japanese engagement. Cultural causation works, in other words, but it turns out it does not have to be the full Western package.

And of course the new Japanese cultural combination immediately applied to the mass education system developed after 1872. Confucian loyalties were explicitly taught, beginning with the valuation of education itself, but so were science and technology and appropriate elements of a culture of innovation.

The Pacific Rim

After Russian and Japanese industrializations, which continued to accelerate during the first half of the twentieth century with obvious wartime and (in Russia's case) revolutionary interruptions, the next set of industrial revolutions did not take shape until the 1950s and 1960s. The focus, then, was on a number of smaller countries in the Pacific Rim, headed by South Korea and Taiwan, but with the city-states of Hong Kong and Singapore participating as well. Of course many other regions, by this point, had some advanced industrial capacity, but mainly in more limited sectors—as, for example, the Brazilian iron and steel industry—as opposed to the economy as a whole. The question of why the Pacific Rim moved forward more distinctively returns us to the inescapable issue of special causation.

The debate mirrors the explanation of the earlier Japanese breakthrough in many respects. But the Pacific Rim countries did feature some particular factors of their own. Each had some special support from Britain or the United States, eager to promote development after the Second World War in the context of Cold War competition. The United States defended South Korea against communist attack in the 1950s, and then poured in substantial economic as well as military assistance. Taiwan, now separate from communist China, housed the United States Pacific fleet, another source of support. Both Singapore and Hong Kong, as remaining outposts of the British Empire, received substantial military and economic development assistance. The importance of special relationships should not be overblown, but they add to the mix of causes.

As in other latecomer industrializations, governments played a vital role in stimulating and guiding early industrialization. Most Pacific Rim countries featured authoritarian states during their early industrialization process, and there was no hesitation in using the power of the State to stimulate growth. Investment was one channel. Korea's State-run Development Bank was providing 45 percent of all investment capital by 1957, while also influencing the policies of private banks. By the same token, governments actively selected industrial sectors that should be targeted for growth. The official Taiwanese economic plan from 1961–4 thus insisted that "heavy industry holds the key to industrialization, as it produces capital goods. We must develop heavy industry so as to support the long-term steady growth of the economy." Governments also helped limit internal competition in industries essential for expansion and export:

thus the Korean government carefully protected two car manufacturers, while also prodding them—ultimately successfully—to develop the technologies and labor efficiencies necessary for successful export. Pacific Rim industrializations, in sum, amply confirmed the significance of effective and intentional government action in spurring the industrial transformation.

The Pacific Rim also maintained its own version of "preindustrial" manufacturing growth. As with Japan, recent scholarship has increasingly emphasized the extent to which industrialization, though a very real change, built on some prior momentum. In the case of Korea, post-Korean War industrialization emerged from a background in which, from 1911 to 1945, the country had been run as a Japanese colony, and unquestionably exploited in the process. But rather unexpectedly it turns out that the same period saw a fairly steady growth in factory industry, designed to help supply Japan and its other colonies. For the Pacific Rim generally, the explosive growth of the Japanese economy provided important markets not only for foods and raw materials, but for factory production as well. Arguably, this offered an equivalent to the "protoindustrial" backdrop so crucial in Western and in Japanese experience.

Finally, of course, there is the question of culture. Headed by Korea—arguably ultimately the country where Confucianism became most thoroughly ingrained—the Pacific Rim overall had extensively embraced Confucianism. The Confucian qualities that may help explain Japanese industrialization, once modified by a new commitment to science, potentially apply to the whole zone. Indeed, as the Pacific Rim joined Japan as the world's second great industrial region, many enthusiasts began to wonder if, in the long run, Confucianism would prove to be an even more effective cultural environment for industrial success than the more individualistic Western version.

For further discussion

(1) Based on your understanding of the primary causes of earlier industrializations, what are the factors you expect to be essential in explaining the Industrial Revolution in Japan?

(2) To what extent was Japanese industrialization a home-grown product, stemming from local factors, as opposed to the result of outside influence and imitation?

(3) To what extent do Japan and Western Europe share a "proto-industrial" experience that explains their ability to industrialize and that contrasts to the patterns in other key regions?

(4) Does the role of the State loom larger in explaining Japanese industrialization than was true for Britain or the West? Or does Japan mainly confirm the newer analysis that emphasizes State involvement?

(5) What factors best explain why Japan industrialized earlier than other parts of Asia?

(6) Compare Confucianism and the modern Western cultural tradition as frameworks for industrialization.

(7) What factors did Pacific Rim countries share with Japan that may help explain their Industrial Revolutions? Or: were the circumstances for economic change in the Pacific Rim so distinctive that a comparison with Japan is misleading?

(8) On balance, were the causes of Japanese and Pacific Rim industrializations similar to those that had spurred Western industrialization, or substantially different?

Further reading

On Japan, see Kaoru Sugihara, *Japan, China and the Growth of the Asian International Economy, 1850–1949* (New York: Oxford University Press, 2005); Steven J. Ericson "Social and Economic Change (1868 to The First World War)," with M. Jones, in *A Companion to Japanese History*, W. M. Tsutsui (ed.) (Malden, MA: Blackwell Publishing Ltd., 2006); Kozo Yamamura, *A Study of Samurai Income and Entrepreneurship: Quantitative Analyses of Economic and Social Aspects of the Samurai in Tokugawa and Meiji Japan* (Cambridge, UK: Cambridge University Press, 1974); and Andrew Fraser, R.H.P. Mason, and Philip Mitchell, *Japan's Early Parliaments, 1880–1905* (New York: Routledge, 1995). See also Tu Wei-ming (ed.), *Confucian Traditions in East Asian Modernity: Moral Education and Economic Culture in Japan and the Four Mini-Dragons* (Cambridge, MA: Harvard University Press, 1996).

On the role of the State, Thomas Smith, *Political Change and Industrial Development in Japan: Government Enterprise: 1868–1880* (Stanford,

CA: Stanford University Press, 1955). On Confucianism, Wei-ming Tu, *Humanity and Self-Cultivation: Essays in Confucian Thought* (Boston, MA: Cheng & Tsui, 1999); on "protoindustrialization" see Akira Hayami and Osamu Saitó, *The Economic History of Japan: 1600–1990: Volume 1: Emergence of Economic Society in Japan, 1600–1859* (New York: Oxford University Press, 2004); Kozo Yamamura, *The Economic Emergence of Modern Japan* (Cambridge, UK: Cambridge University Press, 1997).

On capitalism, see David L. Howell, "The Capitalist Transformation of the Hokkaido Fishery, 1672–1935" (Ph.D. Dissertation, Princeton University, 1989); Eric Jones, *Growth Recurring: Economic Change in World History* (Oxford: Clarendon Press, 1988); and Hung-chao Tai (ed.), *Confucianism and Economic Development: An Oriental Alternative?* (Washington, D.C.: Washington Institute Press, 1989).

On the Pacific Rim, see Alice Amsden, *Asia's Next Giant: South Korea and Late Industrialization* (New York: Oxford University Press, 1989); Ezra Vogel, *Four Little Dragons: The Spread of Industrialization in East Asia* (Cambridge: Harvard University Press, 1990); Dennis McNamara, *The Colonial Origins of Korean Enterprise: 1910–1945* (Cambridge, UK: Cambridge University Press, 2006); Robert Wade, *Governing the Market: Economic Theory and the Role of Government in East Asian Industrialization* (Princeton, NJ: Princeton University Press, 2003); Edwin Winckler and Susan M. Greenhalgh, *Contending Approaches to the Political Economy of Taiwan* (Armonk, NY: M.E.Sharpe, Inc., 1997); Philip West and Frans A.M. Alting Von Geusau, *The Pacific Rim and the Western World: Strategic, Economic, and Cultural Perspectives* (Boulder, CO: Westview Press, 1987).

9

Industrialization of the world, 1990 and onward

After the Pacific Rim industrializations began, a few decades passed before there were further major breakthroughs. Many observers worried that global economic inequality was increasing, because of the gap between the advanced industrial regions and the "developing" world. By the 1990s, however, it was clear that many other countries were beginning to rival the industrial elite, and many regional disparities eased. China was the most obvious case in point, with annual growth rates of 10 percent or more; by 2012 the nation, a massive global source of manufacturing exports, had become the second largest economy in the world, replacing Japan. But Brazil, India, Turkey, Mexico and a number of other countries also laid claim to industrial status.

Specific patterns varied. Brazil had advanced industrial sectors, in areas like steel and computers, but also generated substantial agricultural and raw materials exports. India featured computer software and English-language service sectors, along with some industrial basics. In addition to variety, some debate continued as to whether the industrial emergence would last, or whether it would mature into a full industrial economy. Skeptics about China, for example, pointed to high levels of pollution and potential political and social unrest, as the country faced growing internal economic gaps and tried to combine industrialization with an authoritarian political structure.

On the whole, however, by the second decade of the twenty-first century, the evidence suggested that some form of industrialization had spread to the majority of the world's regions, rather than a privileged few. One result, from the analytical side, was a new set of questions about causation.

First: why were so many regions now able to begin a serious industrialization process? For several reasons, some of the key components necessary to facilitate industrial transformation were becoming easier to acquire. Knowing the factors relevant in explaining Western or Japanese industrial revolutions, scholars can debate the extent to which accessibility has increased, as well as the reasons for this change. But the process may not be uniform: Are some ingredients still harder to replicate, or replace, than others?

Second: comparison remains essential. The varying patterns of contemporary industrializers surely relate in part to different specific causation ingredients. Even more important, despite the global expansion of the process, figuring out why many but not all regions move ahead remains a challenge both for analysis and for economic development policy.

Contemporary industrializations take place in a framework of accelerating global contacts. Exchanges of goods, knowledge, and people flow more freely and rapidly than ever before. This can make industrial transformations more difficult, when competition further threatens local economies or when exploitation of a region's resources increases. On the whole, however, evidence suggests that contemporary globalization favors economic development, providing greater access to necessary knowledge and necessary materials alike. But there is a caution here: we know that, even with great opportunities for imitation, industrialization is a challenging process. It still requires sufficient causation, in any region involved.

Industrial growth before "revolution"

Not surprisingly, most of the recent industrial revolutions have a clear prehistory. This makes sense in two ways. First, industrial models have now been around for two centuries. Many societies, well in advance of full industrialization, began to establish some factories, if only for local production. Limited changes of this sort do not necessarily lead to a fuller transformation, but they can certainly help prepare it. Government, business, and labor all gain some relevant experience. Imitation *within* the society becomes possible. If and when a more wide-ranging industrial revolution does occur, it is clearly connected to the earlier precedents.

And second, we have seen that both in Japan and in Western Europe, there is a strong argument that significant manufacturing growth must precede the real technological breakthroughs. Whether we call the process protoindustrialization or an "industrious" revolution, manufacturing growth creates business and labor skills, and also consumer demand that can help generate the more substantial transformation later on. In many ways, depending on where this factor resides in a causation debate, pilot factories or factory sectors in the recent industrializers replicate the Western or Japanese experience, but simply in a slightly different way.

A tricky aspect of this pattern in many recent industrializers is that its immediate effects on the overall economy are so limited that many observers barely notice that there is some real movement away from traditional operations. Remember that many of the recent cases were listed as "undeveloped" or "third world" until quite recently, as many scholars worried that they might never turn the corner. Now, we can see, important shifts were occurring just beneath the surface, that may help explain the clearer emergence in the 1980s or 1990s. Are there analogies to this situation in the early phases of British or Japanese industrialization, in changes that did not fully register in the overall economy?

Examples abound, from local business ventures, government projects, and foreign investments. The Ford Motor Company set up a plant in Malaysia in 1932, and a foreign shoe firm followed; by the later 1940s there were over 125,000 manufacturing workers in the country. The number of Indonesian factory workers had doubled during the late 1930s, and while some of this was in sectors like food processing, a metalworking segment developed as well. Brazil and Turkey both set up government-run steel operations between the world wars, with Brazil registering particular success. India's steel industry also expanded. Both management experience and worker training gained ground from efforts of this sort. Individual companies displayed a strikingly entrepreneurial spirit, like a Chinese cigarette firm that began to compete against foreign imports even before the

First World War, insisting on the latest technologies and efficiency procedures: its owner proclaimed, "Whoever works in the manufacturing business must have far-sighted vision and cannot be so stingy about insignificant amounts of money [for investment]."

Debate over timing applies to many different countries. Brazil is a clear case in point. Conventional scholarship long identified the gestation period for Brazilian industrialization after the Second World War. Recent historical work however has focused more in the interwar period, and particularly the 1930s dictatorship of Getúlio Vargas. The First World War had interrupted European factory imports to Brazil, creating new demand for local industrial production, and then Vargas committed to greater government support in response to the 1930s Depression. Vargas also used the government to create friendly labor unions, which may also have eased the pre-industrialization process. Many scholars now see this twentieth-century prehistory as crucial to explaining Brazil's more recent economic surge.

China is another much-debated case. This is a country whose earlier manufacturing strength has of course received great attention. More specific analysis applies to the period in the 1960s when Mao Zedong, the communist leader, declared a "great leap forward," emphasizing small scale production in and around individual homes, even in the countryside. The leader hoped to take advantage of the nation's huge population, to push manufacturing in a way different both from the West and from Soviet Russia. Most overall indices suggest that the policy was a failure, with output declining. But more recent scholarship has pointed to opportunities for peasant workers to gain new experience, in ways that would pay off later in business and labor force development. Is this a distinctive example of a now-familiar preparatory pattern?

Local and international factors

Important debate applies to the mixture of local and global impulses in recent industrializations. A policy called import substitution, developing in the Middle East and Latin America between the world wars, and in India after decolonization, played a key role in stimulating factory industry. Governments like Turkey and Argentina slapped high tariffs on common manufactured imports, like textiles or automobiles, in order to encourage local factories. The result could be inefficient production, protected from competition, but the experience might help later on with enhanced labor and business experience. Some scholars argue that import substitution helps explain why many Latin American countries focused early industrialization on meeting domestic demand, with export interests arriving later.

On the other hand, the role of multinational corporations in setting up branches and providing investment capital and state-of-the-art technology must also be considered, even in cases like Brazil or Mexico. Many of the new industrializers did not go it alone. Certainly in many parts of Southeast Asia, multinational companies stimulated considerable activity in the 1950s and 1960s, which in some cases was then later enhanced by government investment activity. They gained a place even in China by the 1990s. Multinationals unquestionably exploited cheap local labor and loose regulations. But did they also improve subsequent capacity to industrialize more fully? How does their role compare to more local stimuli?

This kind of discussion relates closely to the familiar timing issue: did multinationals kick off major changes in Brazil by their 1950s initiatives, or had a development process already begun on a more purely national basis? Conclusions may vary case to case. Some scholars see import substitution as particularly important in Latin America, with international corporations more significant in places like Southeast Asia where industrialization, as a further result, was heavily oriented toward exports. Initial sources of demand, in other words, may vary, in ways that help explain timing and sales preferences alike.

Culture

Did particular belief systems matter as much for recent industrializations as they had in earlier cases? The discussion of the relevance of Confucian heritage obviously continues with Chinese industrial success. Chinese communism had attacked Confucianism in many ways, but a strong heritage remained: did it contribute to the work and education motivations that in turn facilitated the industrial surge?

But cultural adjustments now extended well beyond the Western and Confucian orbits. After all, by the later twentieth century scientific principles and training were widely available, except in the very poorest countries. Literally hundreds of thousands of students regularly received technical training abroad. However these changes might mix with local culture, surely they provided a spur to industrial development comparable, for example, to the Japanese combination of innovation and Confucianism a century before. Turkey might be a case in point. The republic established a new, secular system of education in 1924, and then revamped universities after 1933; in both cases science education received great attention. The result did not eliminate Islamic beliefs in the country, but by the later twentieth century it had clearly established a culture more open to ideas of innovation in the area of business and technology.

Yet debate continues over whether certain cultures may nevertheless discourage major industrial innovation. Religious intolerance measurably increased in some (not all) Islamic countries, sometimes even as scientific training advanced for an elite; would this have an impact on industrial potential? In China, industrial advance continued even amid government-imposed limits on freedom of expression, but might this raise problems later on? Religious clashes in several countries clearly interfered with economic stability and prevented significant change.

Even by the early twenty-first century, were certain cultural patterns "better" for industrialization than others, and how might the role of culture in recent transformations be defined? Is the ability to embrace science the key measure of relevant cultural context by this point?

The State

Considerable discussion applies to the role of the State in recent economic development, reflecting disputes about this issue in earlier industrializations; ongoing scholarly analysis; and some contemporary ideological concerns. The discussion bears also on the local versus international balance, with State efforts adding to internal sources of change.

Industrialization was clearly possible under various late-twentieth–century regimes, from Chinese authoritarianism to more democratic forms in Brazil or India. But some would argue that a more general loosening of the State's role was a key precondition for recent industrializations. China opened to considerable private capitalism, as well as extensive foreign contacts, in 1978, though substantial government economic activity continued. The government also began releasing peasants from the farms, creating huge labor potential much like the nineteenth-century serf emancipation in Russia. There is little question that these changes played a key role in triggering much more rapid industrial growth. India loosened its regulatory apparatus in the early 1990s. In Latin America a spread of democracy preceded the clear industrial boom. Is there a "neo-liberal" model here, linking greater latitude for private enterprise to industrial advance; or are patterns too diverse?

Other scholars continue to insist on the special importance of State initiatives in the most recent versions of latecomer industrialization. Alice Amsden, a development economist, covered the continued importance of government investment allocations, in countries like Turkey and Malaysia, as had previously been the case with the Pacific Rim. Even private investment banks, like the Industrial Finance Corporation in Thailand, offered special rates for government-sponsored projects, Brazil used taxpayer funds in its development bank, targeting iron and chemicals industries. In all these cases, Amsden argues, government selection of growth sectors, and the combination of special funding with requirements for technological innovation, substituted for the kind of competition that had operated in earlier Western industrializations in generating new industries. Brazil's agencies for example directly scrutinized the technological standards of the firms they were targeting. Government selection also favored sectors with high export potential.

China inevitably spurs particular attention to the role of government. If the modification of State control after 1978 helps explain the timing of the industrial surge, there is no question that government intervention remained considerable, and on balance (despite some inefficient State enterprises) helped push the nation toward industrial growth. Richard Conroy emphasizes the distinctive role of the Chinese state in guiding scientific research, and focusing it on supporting industrial innovation. He contrasts this with what he sees as the more separate path of science in the West. It was the Chinese state, then, that tightly linked science and the production process, with direct impact on the rapid growth patterns that emerged by the 1980s.

Debate over the balance between private entrepreneurial effort and government initiative clearly continues. The relationship can also inform analysis of the role of cultural values and prior economic change.

Explaining recent industrializations involves a mix of familiar and novel factors. The role of multinationals has no full prior precedent, though it can be linked to activities of foreign entrepreneurs in places like Belgium or Russia earlier on; and of course it is not always clear whether multinationals help or hinder even now. On the other hand, analysis of pre-revolution manufacturing growth (rural as well as urban), or culture and science, and the balance between private innovation and the role of the State, echo assessments of earlier industrializations. Have contemporary societies simply gained clearer mastery over a standard causation model, or are some really novel factors involved?

For further discussion

(1) How does a formal adoption of import substitution compare with British policy in the later eighteenth century? Can we compare causations in such chronologically separate cases?
(2) Is a debate over culture still relevant to assessing recent causes of industrial change?
(3) Pick a country in which multinational corporations run part of advanced industry either directly or through agents. (Mexico or China would be possibilities, or Indonesia or Vietnam among earlier-stage developers.) To what extent is industrial growth responding to internal factors, to what extent is it simply the product of expanding multinational activity?

(4) Do contemporary conditions make industrial transformations easier than in the past, requiring less elaborate causation? If so, what has changed?

(5) How do governments become sources of basic economic change in recent world history? Is their involvement measurably different from the role of the State in Western industrialization?

(6) What factors should be considered in explaining recent industrializations? Does the list extend beyond prior trajectory, cultural change, and some balance between private business and government stimulation?

(7) Do the factors that explain why recent industrializations have occurred also explain why some regions are not yet fully involved?

Further reading

See Alice Amsden, *The Rise of "The Rest": Challenges to the West from Late-Industrializing Economies* (New York: Oxford University Press, 2001); Nasir Tyabji, *Industrialization and Innovation: The Indian Experience* (Thousand Oaks, CA: Sage Publications, 2000); Gordon White, *Riding the Tiger: The Politics of Economic Reform in Post-Mao China* (Stanford, CA: Stanford University Press, 1993); and Peter N. Stearns, *The Industrial Revolution in World History*, 4/e (Boulder, CO: Westview Press, 2013).

On multinationals, Alfred D. Chandler, Jr., *Scale and Scope: The Dynamics of Industrial Capitalism* (Cambridge, MA: Harvard University Press, 1994); and Bruce Mazlish, *The New Global History* (New York: Routledge, 2006).

On Brazil, see Werner Baer, "Import Substitution and Industrialization in Latin America: Experiences and Interpretations," *Latin American Research Review*, 7, no. 1 (Spring 1972); Warren Dean, *The Industrialization of Sao Paulo, 1880–1945* (Austin and London: University of Texas Press for the Institute of Latin American Studies, 1969); and Jeff Frieden, "Third World Indebted Industrialization: International Finance and State Capitalism in Mexico, Brazil, Algeria and South Korea," *International Organization*, 35, no. 3 (Summer 1981).

Good surveys on China include Richard E. Baldwin, Philippe Martin, and Gianmarco I. P. Ottaviano, "Global Income Divergence, Trade, and Industrialization: The Geography of Growth Take-Offs," *Journal of*

Economic Growth, 6 (March 2001); Ian Bradbury, Richard Kirkbury, and Shen Guanbao, "Development and Environment: The Case of Rural Industrialization and Small-Town Growth in China," *Ambio*, 25 (May 1996); Gregory Clark and David Jacks, "Coal and the Industrial Revolution, 1700–1869," *European Review of Economic History*, 11 (April 2007); Richard Conroy, "Technological Innovation in China's Recent Industrialization," *The China Quarterly*, 97 (March 1984). See also Kenneth Pomeranz, *The Great Divergence: China, Europe, and the Making of the Modern World Economy* (Princeton, NJ: Princeton University Press, 2000); Christine P.W. Wong, "Fiscal Reform and Local Industrialization: The Problematic Sequencing of Reform in Post-Mao China," *Modern China*, 18 (April 1982); and Tim Wright, "An Economic Cycle in Imperial China? Revisiting Robert Hartwell on Iron and Coal," *Journal of the Economic and Social History of the Orient*, 50 (2007): 398–423.

10

For further discussion

The Industrial Revolution and its interaction with world history have now passed the second century mark, but questions persist as to exactly what factors set it in motion and facilitated its expansion. This chapter raises some of the key questions that can organize ongoing analysis. Obviously, a number of additional topics deserve attention, and some have been treated in earlier sections. The goal in this brief conclusion is to continue to sort out the best ways to explain the sources of the Industrial Revolution process and to link these to the revolution's impacts.

Here's a first question: of the major industrial revolutions that have occurred so far, which is the hardest to explain, and why? Is there also an "easiest" case?

Another warm-up: what two or three factors, once seen as quite plausible explanations, have turned out not to work out well? What has been the process of assessing and ultimately discarding factors of this sort?

As you review debates over industrial causation, discuss what kinds of additional data would be most helpful in resolving some of the questions involved.

A number of debates have involved culture, or more specific features of culture like science or economics. Discuss the best ways to construct a cultural causation argument, including evidence of direct connections between culture and industrial change. Assess the role of culture in comparative analysis, both in explaining different specific industrial revolutions and in accounting for regions where industrialization was slow to develop. Finally, return to the periodic claims about the importance of cultural tolerance for economic innovation: what is the most accurate evaluation of this factor?

At various points scholars have discussed the motivations for some of the key actors in industrialization: businessmen, workers, State officials, inventors. Do the debates over industrial causes give enough credit to the human genius involved in early industrial innovations and inventions? What kinds of people have wanted to promote industrialization, and why? What kinds of people have tended to resist or avoid the process? Is an evaluation of motivation a key element in the analysis of industrial causation?

Discuss the impact of contemporary issues on causation debates. Candidates include: ongoing disagreements about the economic role of the state; pride or uncertainty about Western values; the influence of current economic trends in various world regions; a desire to promote greater tolerance. Have contemporary concerns distorted the analysis of causation or have they encouraged fruitful new lines of inquiry?

Pick a region that was or is slow to industrialize, and discuss the factors that seem to be missing. Analyze the balance between internal weaknesses (government, culture, resources, etc.) and external interference or exploitation. If you were advising a contemporary region that has not yet industrialized, what would you recommend that its leaders focus on?

Select one of the factors that show up fairly consistently in causation analysis, such as natural resources, or the State, or education. Lay out the best case for the importance of this factor in explaining several industrial revolutions, but also indicate some of the problems or complexities involved. Is the factor more important in some cases than in others? Has historians' evaluation of the factor changed over time?

Pick another big causation problem in world history, and discuss how the experience of assessing debates over industrial causation might help you figure out appropriate analytical strategies. For example: what kinds of information might prove necessary about historical patterns *prior* to a big change? How can one best balance factors coming from different areas of activity, from population trends to politics to the natural environment? In explaining big changes, is it best to look for two or three striking causes, or an accumulation of smaller ones?

There is a final angle to the analysis of industrial causation that opens another important field for debate. Industrial societies, and their contrasts with more traditional societies, have been evaluated from all sorts of angles. Quite clearly, for example, at least over time, industrial societies improve living standards and facilitate consumerism. Recent industrial growth in places like China and Brazil has been fundamental in reducing global economic inequalities (though not inequalities within societies). Equally clearly, industrialization, unless carefully managed, has adverse impacts on the environment, at least locally and now probably globally. Other impacts, however, are harder to assess. Does industrialization make work, for most people, more or less interesting? Does it worsen or improve family life? Or does it possibly not make much difference despite important specific changes?

Debating the effects of industrialization is an inescapable assignment, for it provides insight into the quality of our own lives and those of people around us. It's also a hard assignment. It involves trying to figure out what evidence is available, for example about changes in the quality of work life. It involves value judgments: industrialization promotes consumerism, but is this a good or a bad thing?

Without artificially limiting the process of evaluation, it is possible to suggest that the kinds of causation analysis historians have undertaken provide at least one relevant vantage point. What kind of problems was industrialization intended to solve, as the process initially took shape, and did it solve them? Could and should some of the causes have been ignored? Was industrialization a triumph of the interests and values of some people over the wider society, or did it meet more general needs? Any big transformation—and industrialization certainly qualifies here—has some unintended consequences. But it is legitimate to anchor an initial assessment in the kinds of issues that prompted the change in the first place. Could industrial revolutions have been avoided, and would we all be better off if they had?

From early industrialization onward, some groups and individuals called for an alternative, a different system. In the nineteenth century, utopians in Europe and the United States set up optional experiments. Later leaders like Mohandas Gandhi in India clearly hoped for a nonindustrial future. Some of the radicals in the 1960s called for an end to many features of industrial society, and some retreated outright to rural communes. The periodic search for a different path deserves real attention. But it is also important to note that, to date, none of the nonindustrial options has ultimately drawn wide support. Whether voluntarily or under duress, most people come to value key aspects of the industrial economy. Does this mean that industrialization sprang from valid interests and needs? How much does a better understanding of what set the whole process in motion help us weigh its ultimate effects?

Index